ASSAULT ON THE AFTERLIFE

SATAN'S WAR AGAINST HEAVEN

END TIMES ARMOR SERIES

ASSAULT ON THE AFTERLIFE
SATAN'S WAR AGAINST HEAVEN

Copyright © 2021 Marsha Kuhnley
Visit the author's website at Rapture911.com

Edited by Drezhn Publishing LLC

All rights reserved. No part of this publication may be reproduced, distributed, or transmitted in any form or by any means, including photocopying, recording, or other electronic or mechanical methods, without the prior written permission of the publisher, except in the case of brief quotations embodied in critical reviews and certain other noncommercial uses permitted by copyright law.

While the author has made every effort to provide accurate internet addresses at the time of publication, neither the publisher nor the author assumes responsibility for errors or changes that occur after publication. The publisher and author do not have any control over and do not assume responsibility for third-party websites or their content.

Published by Drezhn Publishing LLC
PO BOX 67458
Albuquerque, NM 87193-7458

Cover Design by MIBL ART
www.miblart.com

Print Edition - February 2022
Version 1.1

PAPERBACK ISBN: 978-1-947328-54-9
HARDBACK ISBN: 978-1-947328-55-6

Unless otherwise indicated, all Scripture quotations are taken from the World English Bible (WEBP), a public domain translation of the Holy Bible.

Scripture quotations marked (NLT) are taken from the Holy Bible, New Living Translation, copyright © 1996, 2004, 2015 by Tyndale House Foundation. Used by permission of Tyndale House Publishers, Inc., Carol Stream, Illinois 60188. All rights reserved.

Scripture quotations marked (NKJV) are taken from the New King James Version®. Copyright © 1982 by Thomas Nelson. Used by permission. All rights reserved.

Scripture quotations marked (AMP) taken from the Amplified® Bible (AMP), Copyright © 2015 by The Lockman Foundation. Used by permission. www.Lockman.org

TABLE OF CONTENTS

INTRODUCTION - SATAN'S ASSAULT ON THE AFTERLIFE 1
    DEAR READER 2
    END TIMES ARMOR 5

PART 1 - SATAN STARTED A WAR 7
    CHAPTER 1 - SATAN'S FIRST ATTACK 8
        1.1. SATAN'S DECLARATION 10
        1.2. SATAN'S SERPENT 12
    CHAPTER 2 - SATAN'S MOTIVE 14
        2.1. SATAN'S EVIL DESIRES 14
        2.2. SATAN'S JEALOUSY 17
        2.3. SATAN'S PLEASURE 20
    CHAPTER 3 - SATAN'S WARFARE TACTICS 24
        3.1. SATAN STEALS, KILLS, DESTROYS 24
        3.2. SATAN ACCUSES 30
        3.3. SATAN DECEIVES 33
    CHAPTER 4 - SATAN'S WARTIME PROPAGANDA 39

PART 2 - SATAN'S ASSAULT ON HEAVEN 43
    CHAPTER 5 - HEAVEN IS UNDER FIRE 44
        5.1. HEAVEN ISN'T BORING AND BUREAUCRATIC 44
        5.2. HELL ISN'T FUN AND EXCITING 52
        5.3. HOW TO BE SAVED 55
    CHAPTER 6 - BURNING MAN 60
    CHAPTER 7 - BATTLE OF THE GREAT RESET 65

PART 3 - SATAN'S ASSAULT ON THOSE WHO LIVE IN HEAVEN 73
    CHAPTER 8 - DEMONIC COMMUNICATION 74
    CHAPTER 9 - UNANSWERED PRAYERS 83

PART 4 - SATAN'S ASSAULT ON FUTURE CITIZENS OF HEAVEN 91
    CHAPTER 10 - I AM CHRIST 92
    CHAPTER 11 - THE UNDEAD APOCALYPSE 98
    CHAPTER 12 - IT'S JUST A SIMULATION 105
    CHAPTER 13 - A MULTIVERSE OF DO-OVERS 112
    CHAPTER 14 - EVOLVE INTO A TRANSHUMAN 117

  Chapter 15 - Achieve Immortality As A Posthuman 124
  Chapter 16 - Be More Than Human As A Hybrid 132

PART 5 - SATAN'S ASSAULT REACHES A CLIMAX 141
  Chapter 17 - A Return To The Beginning 142
  Chapter 18 - The Afterlife Is Rejected 154

PART 6 - SATAN ALREADY LOST HIS WAR 159
  Chapter 19 - The King Is Coming 160
  Chapter 20 - All Will See 169

SATAN'S WAR AGAINST HEAVEN

ASSAULT ON THE AFTERLIFE

END TIMES ARMOR SERIES

Marsha Kuhnley

INTRODUCTION

SATAN'S ASSAULT ON THE AFTERLIFE

DEAR READER

I need you to know that we are living in the very last of the last days before Jesus returns. The Bible gives us many signs to look for regarding events leading up to Jesus's second coming. Right before Jesus places his feet on the Mount of Olives there's a seven-year tribulation period. It's during that period of time that the Antichrist reigns over the entire earth. He is called the Antichrist because he will be opposed to everything that Christ is. When we can clearly see signs that the tribulation period is about to begin, then we also know that Jesus's second coming is near.

End times signs are abundant today. In my End Times Armor series, a collection of standalone books, I focus on the signs of war. Not what you see on the news regarding nations at war or people groups fighting. I'm referring to the spiritual war we're fighting against Satan. Now, I know that some of you reading this aren't familiar with Satan or this war. That's okay. You're going to learn a lot about both in this book.

In this book, we're going to discuss Satan's assault on the afterlife. You see, the Bible reveals who and what the Antichrist is going to wage war against during his reign. In the Scripture below, the "beast" is the Antichrist, and the "dragon" is Satan.

> I saw a beast coming up out of the sea, having ten horns and seven heads. On his horns were ten crowns, and on his heads, blasphemous names. ... The dragon gave him his power, his throne, and great authority. ... He opened his mouth for blasphemy against God, to blaspheme his name, his dwelling, and those who dwell in heaven. It was given to him to make war with the saints and to overcome them. Authority over every tribe, people, language, and nation was given to him. All who dwell on the earth will worship him, everyone whose name has not been written from the foundation of the world in the book of life of the Lamb who has been killed. (Revelation 13:1-2, 6-8)

> The great dragon was thrown down, the old serpent, he who is called the devil and Satan, the deceiver of the whole world. (Revelation 12:9)

Satan, our arch enemy, is the one who will be behind all of the

Antichrist's actions. He's going to possess the Antichrist, just like he possessed Judas before Judas betrayed Jesus. That's why it's really Satan's assault. The Antichrist is going to blaspheme, show contempt and irreverence, for "God," God's "dwelling," and "those who dwell in heaven." God's dwelling place is, of course, heaven. Those who live in heaven are the holy angels, the deceased Old Testament believers (people God considered righteous before Jesus's crucifixion), and people who died after Jesus's crucifixion who placed their faith in him before they died. But that's not all. If you've placed your faith in Jesus, then you too are a citizen of heaven.

> For our citizenship is in heaven, from where we also wait for a Savior, the Lord Jesus Christ. (Philippians 3:20)

As a citizen of heaven that means you're going to be living there one day. That day is going to happen sooner than you may think. You see, you won't even be on earth when the Antichrist is ruling. You're going to be dwelling in heaven because Jesus is going to remove all believers in an event called the rapture before the tribulation even begins. We're going to talk about the rapture later on in Chapter 19.

What's more is that Jesus desires everyone to come to faith in him and have eternal life. That's exactly why he died! He loves everyone he created and thus he wants everyone to be a citizen of heaven. Throughout this book I refer to people who believe Jesus is their savior as believers or saved.

> God our Savior, who desires all people to be saved and come to full knowledge of the truth. For there is one God and one mediator between God and men, the man Christ Jesus, who gave himself as a ransom for all. (1 Timothy 2:3-6)

If you haven't yet placed your faith in Jesus, you're going to learn how to be saved in Chapter 5. But know that as a potential citizen of heaven that Satan's assault is against you too.

This war just got personal, didn't it? Satan's assault on everything to do with heaven is an assault on the afterlife. Our afterlife. Satan isn't going to start this war once we're all in heaven and the Antichrist is reigning. No. He started his war against heaven a very long time ago when he lived in heaven and rebelled against God. His first attack against us and our afterlife happened in the garden of Eden. The climax of his war happens during the tribulation period. You'll learn about that in Chapter 17. Since that period is so very near, you must understand that Satan's assault on the afterlife is raging today.

Throughout this book we're going to look at how Satan is assaulting the afterlife, why he picked this fight in particular, and how you can identify his deceptive tactics and know the truth. This isn't any ordinary book about heaven and what all the different religions say about it. Quite the contrary actually! That's been done before and there are plenty of books out there you can read to educate yourself about that. Instead, I'm going to expose Satan's war in areas you've never even realized were an assault on the afterlife. Just take a peek at the chapter titles and you'll get a good sense of what we're going to cover.

Before we can begin, you need to equip yourself to fight in this battle. That's right. You're going to learn that it's time for you to take a stand and be prepared to wield the Sword of Truth. Get your armor on, we're at war!

Marsha

END TIMES ARMOR

We are in a war. This isn't an ordinary war with typical weapons where land and resources are at stake. No, this is a spiritual war involving demonic rulers. What's at stake is the most precious thing of all: your soul.

The apostle Paul tells us about this war in Ephesians chapter 6:

> Finally, be strong in the Lord and in the strength of his might. Put on the whole armor of God, that you may be able to stand against the wiles of the devil. For our wrestling is not against flesh and blood, but against the principalities, against the powers, against the world's rulers of the darkness of this age, and against the spiritual forces of wickedness in the heavenly places. Therefore put on the whole armor of God, that you may be able to withstand in the evil day, and having done all, to stand. Stand therefore, having the utility belt of truth buckled around your waist, and having put on the breastplate of righteousness, and having fitted your feet with the preparation of the Good News of peace, above all, taking up the shield of faith, with which you will be able to quench all the fiery darts of the evil one. And take the helmet of salvation, and the sword of the Spirit, which is the word of God; with all prayer and requests, praying at all times in the Spirit, and being watchful to this end in all perseverance and requests for all the saints. (Ephesians 6:10-18)

Paul tells us who we are and aren't fighting in this war. We aren't fighting "flesh and blood" means it's not a war against people, since people are made of flesh and blood. This means your unbelieving neighbor who disagrees with you on the key issues today isn't your enemy. This is a war against the wiles or strategies of "the devil." Satan is the devil. That's right. Satan is very real and he's your enemy. You're going to learn more about him throughout this book. You need to know that he's the General of the "principalities," "powers," "rulers of the darkness," and the "spiritual forces of wickedness." Please remember that your fellow humans aren't the enemy. We are living in spiritually dark times where many people are imprisoned by Satan and his lies. Your goal should be to rescue them, not attack them.

Since our enemy is spiritual, we must use spiritual means to both protect and defend ourselves. This is our End Times Armor. This armor isn't ordinary armor of leather or chain mail. It's the "armor of God." Let's look at the elements in this armor. The "belt of truth" is God's Word. You need to know your Bible. Have it stored in your heart and close to you, ready to use it like a tool you'd pull out of a utility belt. The "breastplate of righteousness" is you placing your faith in Jesus. He's the one who makes you righteous. Having "fitted your feet" with the gospel means you're able to demonstrate your faith in both words and actions. The "shield of faith" is you knowing and calling on all the promises of God when Satan's attack comes against you. Do not be afraid. Have hope. Your "helmet of salvation" is being fully confident that you have been saved through your faith in Jesus. You are sealed with the Holy Spirit.

I want you to notice that God gave you a weapon as well. He expects you to use it. The "sword of the Spirit" is your weapon. It's the Word of God. When Satan came against Jesus to tempt him in the wilderness, Jesus combated Satan's lies with Scripture (Matthew 4; Luke 4). There is power in the Word of God. Use it.

> For the word of God is living and active, and sharper than any two-edged sword, piercing even to the dividing of soul and spirit, of both joints and marrow, and is able to discern the thoughts and intentions of the heart. (Hebrews 4:12)

After we've put on our armor, Paul tells us we need to pray at all times. We need to be close to God in order to draw strength from him. We get close to God by talking to God and reading his Word.

The last thought I want to leave with you is the expectation God has put on us to take action. There's a purpose for wearing armor. It's to protect us in the battle. That means we're supposed to be engaged in the battle. Look at how many times God used the word or variation of the word *stand* in the first Scripture. I counted four times. It doesn't say put on God's armor and sit and watch what happens. No, it says stand! This means rise up, hold your ground, hold your position, endure, and display courage and strength.

We're living in one of the most exciting times in all of history. Put on your armor and stand with me in this battle!

PART 1

SATAN STARTED A WAR

CHAPTER 1 - SATAN'S FIRST ATTACK

Before we can discuss how this assault on the afterlife started, I need to make sure we're all on the same page regarding who God is and who Satan is. There's a lot of confusion and deception about them these days.

Let's start with God. You need to know he's the only God in existence.

> Remember the former things of old; for I am God, and there is no other. I am God, and there is none like me. I declare the end from the beginning, and from ancient times things that are not yet done. I say: My counsel will stand, and I will do all that I please. (Isaiah 46:9-10)

God proves that fact by declaring "the end from the beginning." That means he does it with Bible prophecy. God created everything, including time, thus he knows the future. Now, don't confuse God with a puppet master. You know you have free will because you make countless choices all the time. It's that God operates outside of time and already knows all the choices each of us will make. This demonstrates that God is omniscient or possessing infinite knowledge (Psalm 147:5). The Bible is the Word of God and it's full of prophecy. In fact, almost one-third of the Bible is prophetic.[1] God is trustworthy because his prophecies come true. He likes to use prophecy because when we see things that God spoke about long ago come true, it grows our faith. If you want to learn more about why you can trust God and the Bible because of fulfilled prophecy, read Part 6 in my book *Rapture 911: What To Do If You're Left Behind*.[2]

God created everything. Literally everything. That includes the earth, the heavens, the sun, the stars, the angels, animals, plants, and mankind (Genesis 1). This reveals that God is all-powerful or omnipotent (Jeremiah 32:17, 27). God is also present everywhere all the time, or omnipresent (Psalm 139:1-18). There is nowhere you can go to escape from God's Spirit. God sees everything, so nothing is hidden from him. I need to point out that just because God created everything that doesn't mean that everything is part of God, is holy, and deserves to be worshiped. That's false teaching and idolatry right there. We are not to worship anything God created. We are to worship God only (Exodus 20:1-5).

There are many descriptions of God in the Bible. They all reveal his character: Yahweh or LORD (Genesis 2:4), Father (Matthew 23:9), Creator (Genesis 1:1), Almighty (Revelation 1:8), I AM (Exodus 3:14), Everlasting (Genesis 21:33), Just (Acts 22:14), Merciful (Jeremiah 3:12), Refuge (Psalm 91:2), and Love (1 John 4:8). The Trinity is a way to describe the three key ways that God manifests himself: as God, as Jesus, and as the Holy Spirit (Matthew 28:18-19). Now, there's only one God, not three different Gods. Remember that God is almighty and can do anything. Nothing is impossible for him. He can manifest however he wants to. As a Spirit (1 Corinthians 2:7-16), as a man (Philippians 2:5-11), as a light (Revelation 21:23), as a burning bush (Exodus 3:2), or as a pillar of cloud (Exodus 13:21) for example.

Let's move on to Satan. He's an angel. He is known by many names and descriptions in the Bible: adversary (1 Peter 5:8), serpent (Genesis 3), devil (Matthew 4), accuser (Revelation 12:10), father of lies (John 8:44), murderer (John 8:44), deceiver (Revelation 12:9), an angel of the light (2 Corinthians 11:14), dragon (Rev 12:9), and god of this world (2 Corinthians 4:4). He used to be "the anointed cherub who covers" or as the NLT translation indicates "the mighty angelic guardian." God named him Lucifer (Isaiah 14:12). He is beautiful, full of wisdom, was a leader of angels, and was perfect in everything he did, until one day. We'll discuss what happened that day in a bit.

> "You were the seal of full measure, full of wisdom, and perfect in beauty. You were in Eden, the garden of God. Every precious stone adorned you: ruby, topaz, emerald, chrysolite, onyx, jasper, sapphire, turquoise, and beryl. Gold work of tambourines and of pipes was in you. They were prepared in the day that you were created. You were the anointed cherub who covers. Then I set you up on the holy mountain of God. You have walked up and down in the middle of the stones of fire. You were perfect in your ways from the day that you were created, until unrighteousness was found in you." (Ezekiel 28:12-15)

This Scripture below tells us that God created everything in the "heavenly realms," the "unseen world." So, God created Satan just as he created all the other angels.

> Christ is the visible image of the invisible God. He existed before anything

was created and is supreme over all creation, for through him God created everything in the heavenly realms and on earth. He made the things we can see and the things we can't see—such as thrones, kingdoms, rulers, and authorities in the unseen world. Everything was created through him and for him. (Colossians 1:15-16 NLT)

As you can see, Satan is not God's brother or opposite. He's also not the brother of Jesus. Jesus isn't an angel. Jesus Christ is "the visible image of the invisible God" meaning God in the flesh. Satan also isn't the ruler of hell, that would be God. God created hell for Satan and his evil angels (Matthew 25:41). God is the only one who has the authority to send angels or people there.

1.1. SATAN'S DECLARATION

So, what happened to Satan? Well, in every war there's always a first assault. In Satan's war against heaven, you probably guessed correctly that Satan threw the first punch. These verses below tell us that one day Satan, who is the "shining one, son of the dawn," said in his "heart." He became full of pride.

> How you have fallen from heaven, shining one, son of the dawn! How you are cut down to the ground, who laid the nations low! You said in your heart, "I will ascend into heaven! I will exalt my throne above the stars of God! I will sit on the mountain of assembly, in the far north! I will ascend above the heights of the clouds! I will make myself like the Most High!" (Isaiah 14:12-14)

Every single one of Satan's "I will" statements is an assault on heaven. He wanted to ascend upward in heaven, exalt his throne above God, sit on God's mountain, ascend above the heights, and be like God himself. His goal is to dethrone God and take over heaven. Satan didn't just think this in his heart. He believed he could achieve it (and he still does!) and started a war. As an authority in heaven, he was able to convince other angels to join him in his war against God and God's holy angels. In fact, he drew "one third of the stars" or angels with him.

> Another sign was seen in heaven. Behold, a great red dragon, having

seven heads and ten horns, and on his heads seven crowns. His tail drew one third of the stars of the sky, and threw them to the earth. ... There was war in the sky. Michael and his angels made war on the dragon. The dragon and his angels made war. They didn't prevail. No place was found for them any more in heaven. The great dragon was thrown down, the old serpent, he who is called the devil and Satan, the deceiver of the whole world. He was thrown down to the earth, and his angels were thrown down with him. (Revelation 12:3-4, 7-9)

While the Scripture above depicts Satan's ultimate banishment from heaven, Satan did get kicked out of heaven and thrown down to earth. Jesus said he saw Satan fall like lightning (Luke 10:18). The Bible doesn't tell us how long Satan was perfect in his ways and faithfully served God before he sinned. We can imagine it must have been a while though. How else would he have been perfect in his ways if he hadn't served for a while? What we do know is that all of God's angels, "sons of God" below, were present when he created the earth and mankind.

> "Where were you when I laid the foundations of the earth? ... When the morning stars sang together, and all the sons of God shouted for joy?" (Job 38:4, 7)

This Scripture above tells us that all of the angels rejoiced when God created the foundations of the earth. They were all happy about it, including Lucifer. That means Lucifer hadn't sinned yet. In fact, some verses we looked at earlier, Ezekiel 28:12-15, tell us that Lucifer was in the garden of Eden, adorned with all sorts of precious stones, and served God. Lucifer must have served God in the garden of Eden for quite some time before he sinned and before Adam was created.

Now, I know you might be a bit confused about the timing of this since we know God created the earth and everything in it in seven days. This is outside the scope of this book, but there are Bible scholars who point out that there's an unknown gap in time between Genesis 1:1, when God created the heavens and earth, and Genesis 1:2 when the earth became without form, void, and dark. They make a very convincing biblical argument that the angels inhabited the earth prior to mankind. Why else would Satan desire to ascend into heaven so much? If he already lived there all the time then he wouldn't long for it now, would he? When Satan and the other fallen angels got kicked out of heaven, God sent judgments upon the earth where he banished them to (Job 9:4-7). That's how the earth became formless, void, and dark. Jack Langford had a really informative series of articles on this in *The Prophecy Watcher* magazine starting in January 2021.[3]

1.2. SATAN'S SERPENT

So now fast forward to Satan sinning, starting a war, and getting kicked out of heaven. He's back on earth again and he sees Adam in the garden of Eden with all sorts of responsibilities to take care of it and the animals (Genesis 2:15-20). This is the very garden that Lucifer once served God in. How do you think Satan felt about that? Do you think Satan was jealous, felt usurped? I bet he did! How much more so since Adam was created in the very image of God? Satan absolutely hated Adam! Now, this is where we enter his war.

God gave Adam, "the man," one command to follow. Let's look at it.

> Yahweh God commanded the man, saying, "You may freely eat of every tree of the garden; but you shall not eat of the tree of the knowledge of good and evil; for in the day that you eat of it, you will surely die." (Genesis 2:16-17)

The punishment for not following the command was death. I wonder if Adam really understood what that meant. He lived in a world without sin and without the curse. God cursed all of creation with decay and death after Adam sinned. So that means there wasn't any of those things when Adam received this rule. God created Eve after giving Adam this command. So, we can assume it was up to Adam to pass along this rule to Eve. Satan's assault on mankind started with this one rule that Adam and Eve likely didn't really understand the consequence of violating.

Here's what Satan did. He was disguised as "the serpent."

> Now the serpent was more subtle than any animal of the field which Yahweh God had made. He said to the woman, "Has God really said, 'You shall not eat of any tree of the garden'?" The woman said to the serpent,

> "We may eat fruit from the trees of the garden, but not the fruit of the tree which is in the middle of the garden. God has said, 'You shall not eat of it. You shall not touch it, lest you die.'" The serpent said to the woman, "You won't really die, for God knows that in the day you eat it, your eyes will be opened, and you will be like God, knowing good and evil." When the woman saw that the tree was good for food, and that it was a delight to the eyes, and that the tree was to be desired to make one wise, she took some of its fruit, and ate. Then she gave some to her husband with her, and he ate it, too. (Genesis 3:1-6)

Satan's first lie to Eve was "you won't really die." His first attack was an assault on the afterlife! Satan's second lie was "you will be like God." This was yet another assault on the afterlife because God is the ruler of heaven. There is no other. Satan told Eve she could have the very same thing that he himself desired: to be like God. Eve was convinced that God was keeping something good from her, so she ate the forbidden fruit.

Adam and Eve did eventually die. Adam died when he was 930 years old (Genesis 5:5). The Bible tells us that to God one day is as a thousand years, and a thousand years as a day (2 Peter 3:8). Since Adam died before he reached 1,000 years old, to God he really did die in a day, just as he said.

Satan knows that if he can get us to doubt God in just one thing then it'll open the door for us to question everything we believe. Doubt is one of Satan's key weapons in this war, and it infects everything today. We'll examine Satan's warfare tactics in Chapter 3. First, let's discuss Satan's motive for assaulting the afterlife in more detail.

CHAPTER 2 - SATAN'S MOTIVE

Have you ever wondered why Satan has waged war against God and heaven? Is it just because he's evil? Perhaps he really thinks he can win against God? If we're to participate successfully in this war, then it's important we understand our enemy's motive. Well, you don't have to wonder any longer. The Bible tells us everything we need to know regarding Satan's purpose in continuing to fight his war that assaults our afterlife.

> What is causing the quarrels and fights among you? Don't they come from the evil desires at war within you? You want what you don't have, so you scheme and kill to get it. You are jealous of what others have, but you can't get it, so you fight and wage war to take it away from them. Yet you don't have what you want because you don't ask God for it. And even when you ask, you don't get it because your motives are all wrong—you want only what will give you pleasure. You adulterers! Don't you realize that friendship with the world makes you an enemy of God? (James 4:1-4 NLT)

There are three main things we can learn about Satan's motive from the Scripture above. First, his motive comes from "evil desires." Second, he's "jealous of what others have." Lastly, his "motives are all wrong" because he only wants what will give him "pleasure." Let's examine each of these in more detail.

2.1. SATAN'S EVIL DESIRES

What do you think Satan's primary evil desire is? Yep, you guessed it correctly. He wants to be God!

> How you have fallen from heaven, shining one, son of the dawn! How you are cut down to the ground, who laid the nations low! You said in your heart, "I will ascend into heaven! I will exalt my throne above the stars of God! I will sit on the mountain of assembly, in the far north! I will ascend above the heights of the clouds! I will make myself like the Most High!" (Isaiah 14:12-14)

We can see in these verses that Satan, the "shining one," desired to be the ruler of heaven. It's interesting to note that Satan already had a throne since he wanted to "exalt" or raise his throne above. The authority that God blessed him with wasn't enough for him. So, what is it about God's throne in particular that Satan desires?

> Yahweh has established his throne in the heavens. His kingdom rules over all. (Psalm 103:19)

God's throne is in heaven. So, Satan wants his permanent home to be in heaven. God also "rules over all." We already established that's what Satan ultimately wants too. But there's a lot more to God's authority than those two things. Have a look at these verses in which Jesus's disciple John is given a glimpse of God's throne room.

> And instantly I was in the Spirit, and I saw a throne in heaven and someone sitting on it. The one sitting on the throne was as brilliant as gemstones—like jasper and carnelian. ... Then I looked again, and I heard the voices of thousands and millions of angels around the throne and of the living beings and the elders. And they sang in a mighty chorus: "Worthy is the Lamb who was slaughtered—to receive power and riches and wisdom and strength and honor and glory and blessing." And then I heard every creature in heaven and on earth and under the earth and in the sea. They sang: "Blessing and honor and glory and power belong to the one sitting on the throne and to the Lamb forever and ever." And the four living beings said, "Amen!" And the twenty-four elders fell down and worshiped the Lamb. (Revelation 4:2-3, 5:11-14 NLT)

Here, we learn that God is worshiped in heaven. He's worshiped by the people who live there with him as noted by the "elders." He's worshiped by "the living beings" who surround his throne. He's also worshiped by "thousands and millions of angels." And "every creature" in heaven, on earth, in the sea, and even under the earth worship God. Essentially, everything God created worships him. This is what Satan's evil desire includes. Satan wants to be worshiped by everyone.

You may recall that Satan tempted Jesus with this in the wilderness.

> The devil took him to an exceedingly high mountain, and showed him all

> the kingdoms of the world and their glory. He said to him, "I will give you all of these things, if you will fall down and worship me." Then Jesus said to him, "Get behind me, Satan! For it is written, 'You shall worship the Lord your God, and you shall serve him only.' " (Matthew 4:8-10)

Satan wanted Jesus, who is God in the flesh and the one who created him, to worship him! During the tribulation period this will turn into a major assault on your afterlife when Satan's man, the Antichrist, declares himself God and then demands everyone on the planet worship him (Revelation 13).

Here's another thing we can glean about Satan's motive since we know he wants to be the ruler of heaven. Rulers pronounce judgment. They're the final say on matters brought before them. Satan wants that power. He wants to be the judge.

Well, the Bible tells us that Jesus has been appointed by God to be the judge of everyone.

> And he ordered us to preach everywhere and to testify that Jesus is the one appointed by God to be the judge of all—the living and the dead. (Acts 10:42 NLT)

I think Satan is particularly angry about this because God has already pronounced judgment on him, it's just a matter of having his sentence carried out. Satan is doomed to the lake of fire that God created for all the fallen angels (Revelation 20:10). Of course, Satan doesn't want that to happen, so he wages war against the ruler of heaven so that he can decide his own fate. Here's another little tidbit the Bible reveals about judgment.

> Don't you know that the saints will judge the world? And if the world is judged by you, are you unworthy to judge the smallest matters? Don't you know that we will judge angels? (1 Corinthians 6:2-3)

The apostle Paul tells us that we, people who've put our faith in Jesus, are going to judge angels. Wow! Now, we don't get to judge Satan, that's all Jesus. Still, I bet this one has Satan furious. That's because the Bible reveals that we were created a little bit lower in status than the angels (Psalm 8:5). Yet God has promised us this authority in the future, in our afterlife. Thus, Satan assaults it.

2.2. SATAN'S JEALOUSY

Now that we've discovered what Satan's evil desires are, let's look at what Satan is jealous of. First and foremost, he's jealous of God. We've already established that he wants to be God.

Next, he's jealous of Jesus. That's because God the father has given Jesus everything that Satan desires. Jesus is God in the flesh, the ruler of heaven and earth, the king of kings, the judge of all creation, and the heir of all things. Hebrews chapter 1 is full of these truths and packs a big punch to Satan. Here are some key points.

> God ... has at the end of these days spoken to us by his Son, whom he appointed heir of all things. ... When he had by himself purified us of our sins, sat down on the right hand of the Majesty on high, having become as much better than the angels. ... For to which of the angels did he say at any time, "You are my Son. Today I have become your father?" ... But of the Son he says, "Your throne, O God, is forever and ever. ... Your years won't fail." But which of the angels has he told at any time, "Sit at my right hand, until I make your enemies the footstool of your feet?" Aren't they all serving spirits, sent out to do service for the sake of those who will inherit salvation? (Hebrews 1:1-5, 8, 12-14)

Satan wants to be the heir of all things. Perhaps he thinks that God can die, and that he's not eternal. Well, these verses make it clear that Jesus's throne is forever and that his years won't fail. Although God did create Satan, he's not God's son, who is equal in all things to God. This Scripture also tells us that the angels were created to serve those who will inherit salvation. Here's another reason why Satan assaults our afterlife. We're the ones who inherit salvation!

> The Spirit himself testifies with our spirit that we are children of God; and if children, then heirs—heirs of God and joint heirs with Christ. (Romans 8:16-17)

This brings me to the third thing Satan is jealous of—us. If we look at the situation from his perspective, we can clearly see that he has a lot of reasons to envy us. When we put our faith in Jesus, we really are very blessed.

Let's start at the beginning of our creation. When God created mankind, he created us in his own image.

> God said, "Let's make man in our image, after our likeness. Let them have dominion over the fish of the sea, and over the birds of the sky, and over the livestock, and over all the earth, and over every creeping thing that creeps on the earth." (Genesis 1:26)

That means we look like God. And we know what God looks like. He looks like Jesus because he is God in the flesh (Colossians 1:15). Jesus has always existed. He was the author of all creation, including the angels (John 1). We were created after Satan started his war in heaven. So, how do you think Satan felt when God created us? You know he was absolutely furious! He wants to be like God and here we were a new creation that looked exactly like God.

On top of that, God gave us a job to do. He told us to have dominion over the earth. Remember from an earlier chapter that I and other Bible scholars believe the angels lived on earth before we did, but then Satan and the fallen angels ruined it (Ezekiel 28:13, Isaiah 14:17). God then took the formless and dark earth and fixed it up for us. Well, how jealous do you think Satan is that God did all that for us? That we essentially got a job that Satan and his fallen angels were fired from? You know I think this also easily explains why Satan is currently the god of this world and has the title deed to the planet (2 Corinthians 4:4). It's because earth was his before it was Adam's. When Adam sinned, it reverted back to Satan. It's also why Satan was able to tempt Jesus with rulership over all the kingdoms of earth (Matthew 4:8-10).

Now, we only lost dominion of the earth temporarily. Jesus won it back when he died on the cross for our sins. When Jesus returns at his second coming, he's going to rule on earth for forever. In fact, we get to rule with him (Revelation 20:6). After the literal millennium passes, God is going to make a brand-new earth for us (Revelation 21). One that won't be messed up by fallen angels, us, sin, and the curse. It'll be glorious! No wonder Satan is jealous of us.

There's another reason Satan and the fallen angels are jealous of us. We get to marry and have children. They don't.

> For when they will rise from the dead, they neither marry nor are given in marriage, but are like angels in heaven. (Mark 12:25)

I know what you're thinking. The angels can't possibly be jealous about this. They can't have kids. All the angels are male. Even if there are female angels, you doubt any of the angels have the physical parts that make having children possible. So, you think this is a non-issue. Not the case! In fact, this is a big deal.

> So the LORD God said to the serpent: "Because you have done this, You [are] cursed ... And I will put enmity Between you and the woman, And between your seed and her Seed; He shall bruise your head, And you shall bruise His heel." (Genesis 3:14-15 NKJV)

In the Scripture above, God is talking to Adam, Eve, and Satan (the "serpent"). This is right after Adam and Eve sinned by eating the forbidden fruit. God mentions the woman's seed and Satan's seed. That refers to exactly what you think it does—offspring. Now, you're probably thinking this could be a spiritual reference. That it's referring to people who have the spirit of Satan, not his literal offspring. Well, in the original Hebrew, the same word for *seed* is used to refer to both the woman and Satan. The woman certainly doesn't have a spirit that's going to be against Satan. So, it must be literal. You may think this is really farfetched, but I'm telling you this is most certainly going to manifest during the tribulation period, and you're going to learn how in Part 4.

Here's some additional biblical proof that angels desire and can attain literal offspring. In the first Scripture below, "God's son's" refers to angels. It's the same term that's used in the book of Job that refers to the angels.

> When men began to multiply on the surface of the ground, and daughters were born to them, God's sons saw that men's daughters were beautiful, and they took any that they wanted for themselves as wives. ... The Nephilim were in the earth in those days, and also after that, when God's sons came in to men's daughters and had children with them. Those were the mighty men who were of old, men of renown. (Genesis 6:1-2, 4)

> Angels who didn't keep their first domain, but deserted their own

dwelling place, he has kept in everlasting bonds under darkness for the judgment of the great day. (Jude 1:6)

Before the flood, some wicked angels decided to leave heaven, "their first domain," so that they could procreate with human women. The result was the "Nephilim," also known as the giants. There's a reason God wanted the Israelites to destroy all the giants who lived in the promised land. They weren't human! They were angel-human hybrids, an abomination to God, beings that couldn't be redeemed. This is also why God sent the flood to destroy almost of all his creation. It was to destroy all the hybrids that the fallen angels created. I believe Satan had a hand in what these angels did. He likely convinced them to do it because they'd get to be like us, and at the same time perhaps prevent his predicted demise by polluting the gene pool and preventing the birth of Jesus. Now, the Bible tells us that the angels who committed that sin already got punished. For that reason, I don't believe Satan himself has committed this sin yet. But he wants to. If for no other reason than to pollute our race and keep us from obtaining salvation. However, since he wants to be God, he desires to have a son like God does. And he will. We know him as the Antichrist.

2.3. SATAN'S PLEASURE

We started this chapter discussing Satan's motives and learned that James 4:1-4 reveals that our motives come from our evil desires, jealousy, and because we want to bring ourselves pleasure. We've addressed the first two, so now let's talk about Satan's desire for pleasure.

> Your rich commerce led you to violence, and you sinned. So I banished you in disgrace from the mountain of God. I expelled you, O mighty guardian, from your place among the stones of fire. Your heart was filled with pride because of all your beauty. Your wisdom was corrupted by your love of splendor. So I threw you to the ground and exposed you to the curious gaze of kings. (Ezekiel 28:16-17 NLT)

These verses shed some light on what gives Satan pleasure. The first thing that's mentioned is his "rich commerce." He's so passionate about it that it led him to violence. *Commerce* is the act of buying and selling stuff. Satan is the master of this. He wants to own it all—all of heaven and all of earth. We already know he has jealousy issues. So, it makes since that when he wants something, he'll do anything to get it, including kill for it. After all, he wants to be the ruler of heaven, and he's waged a war that's lasted thousands of years so that he might achieve it.

The next thing he gets pleasure from is himself. He's beautiful and his heart is filled with pride because of that. I wonder if Satan thinks he deserves to be God because he considers himself more beautiful than Jesus. We know that Jesus didn't have any physical qualities that would make us attracted to him or us desire to worship him (Isaiah 53:2). Satan thinks he deserves to be worshiped because of his beauty.

Satan really thinks he can win his war against God and our afterlife. Let's wrap up this chapter by considering some other reasons why Satan's pride has blinded him to his fate. First, Satan isn't all-knowing like God is. That means Satan doesn't know God's plan until God decides to reveal it. We have the benefit of the entire Bible. When Satan started this war, the Bible didn't exist. Satan didn't know God's plan. He didn't know how he was going to be defeated. He only had the words of God from Genesis chapter 3 to go by. That the woman's seed would be his demise. So, he sought to destroy her seed.

Second, Satan gained the power of death when he got Adam and Eve to eat the forbidden fruit. This victory further swelled his pride. Satan knows he can conquer mankind if he keeps us ensnared in sin and away from knowing Jesus.

> Because God's children are human beings—made of flesh and blood—the Son also became flesh and blood. For only as a human being could he die, and only by dying could he break the power of the devil, who had the power of death. (Hebrews 2:14 NLT)

We know that Jesus defeated death when he was crucified. This reveals another fact about Satan. Even though he's the most intelligent angel God created, he only has what the Bible calls earthly wisdom. We believers on the other hand have the mind of Christ which enables us to understand God's plan (1 Corinthians 2:5-16). If Satan really understood what God revealed in the Old Testament, he never would have let Jesus be crucified. Even before the crucifixion, Satan tried to use his power over death to tempt Jesus into jumping off the top of the temple (Matthew 4:5-7). Satan quoted Scripture that said the angels would protect Jesus, but Satan really hoped they wouldn't. He wanted Jesus to die.

Once Jesus rose from the dead, why did Satan keep up this war when he knew he'd been defeated? Well, that's the key. Satan doesn't believe he's been defeated. He thinks God is a liar. He said so in the garden of Eden when he was tempting Eve (Genesis 3:1-6). He told her that God was lying about the fruit she wasn't supposed to eat. He told her that God lied to her about what would happen if she ate it. That she wouldn't really die. He told her that God lied to her about the fruit's purpose, and that it would give her knowledge that would make her like God.

I wonder if Satan really believes that God created him. Perhaps he thinks there was another God who created God and thus he can attain Godhood too. Doubt is a big motivator for Satan. Going hand in hand with this is that Satan likely doubts that God is all-powerful. There's a possibility he thinks God's power has diminished over time. This is essentially the first law of thermodynamics at play. That law states that energy in a closed system can't be created or destroyed. That it can only change form. The law states there's a finite amount of energy in any closed system. Some scientists believe the universe is a closed system. What if Satan believes God and his creation are a closed system? If Satan believes that God is part of his creation and that a part of God is transferred into what he creates, then Satan would think God isn't fully God anymore. With this mindset, Satan would think he could one day overpower God and take over. Especially if Satan was getting more skilled and proficient in his ways, and amassing more wealth, power, and influence among the angels. He also probably thinks he's evolving into a god. Of course, we know this isn't true. God isn't part of his creation. He's completely separate from it. God is the creator and thus he's constantly creating new things. The universe is an open, infinite system, just like God is infinite. God doesn't ever change (Hebrews 13:8).

How did Satan become so blinded to the truth when it is really obvious to us? Well, one reason is that his pride has deceived him (Obadiah 1:3). Another is that he's just plain blind. It's why he's able to blind the minds of unbelievers (2 Corinthians 4:4). I like how these verses describe how he became blind. Satan's mind has been seared "as with a hot iron."

> But the Spirit says expressly that in later times some will fall away from the faith, paying attention to seducing spirits and doctrines of demons, through the hypocrisy of men who speak lies, branded in their own conscience as with a hot iron. (1 Timothy 4:1-2)

If your brain had been seared with a hot iron, you wouldn't be able to think clearly, either. And this Scripture below tells us how his brain became seared.

> For the wrath of God is revealed from heaven against all ungodliness and unrighteousness of men who suppress the truth in unrighteousness, because that which is known of God is revealed in them, for God revealed it to them. For the invisible things of him since the creation of the world are clearly seen, being perceived through the things that are made, even his everlasting power and divinity, that they may be without excuse. Because knowing God, they didn't glorify him as God, and didn't give thanks, but became vain in their reasoning, and their senseless heart was darkened. Professing themselves to be wise, they became fools. ... Even as they refused to have God in their knowledge, God gave them up to a reprobate mind. (Romans 1:18-22, 28)

Satan knew God intimately. God's power was made obvious to him. But Satan refused to worship God. So, God let his heart be "darkened," he became a "fool," and he was given a "reprobate mind." *Reprobate* means unfit, depraved, morally corrupt, unworthy. I can't help but compare Satan to the scarecrow from *The Wizard of Oz*.[1] Neither one of them have a brain.

We've examined a lot of reasons why Satan assaults the afterlife. Everyone one of these motives is key to understanding how we fight. That's the next topic we're going to address—Satan's warfare tactics. Let's get started.

CHAPTER 3 - SATAN'S WARFARE TACTICS

In this chapter, we're going to focus on how Satan wages war. Of course, Satan uses people to accomplish his purposes, but I need you to remember that people are not your enemy. Your enemy is Satan and his fallen angels.

> For our wrestling is not against flesh and blood, but against the principalities, against the powers, against the world's rulers of the darkness of this age, and against the spiritual forces of wickedness in the heavenly places. (Ephesians 6:12)

We can learn all that we need to know about Satan's warfare tactics by carefully examining his activities in the Bible and the descriptions of his character. There are three traits in particular that we're going to discuss. The first is that Satan steals, kills, and destroys. The next is that Satan is the accuser. Lastly, we'll cover Satan being the master deceiver.

3.1. SATAN STEALS, KILLS, DESTROYS

Let's begin. In the first two Scriptures below, Jesus is the one speaking. The last verse was written by Jesus's disciple Peter.

> The thief only comes to steal, kill, and destroy. (John 10:10)

> You are of your father the devil, and you want to do the desires of your father. He was a murderer from the beginning. (John 8:44)

> Be sober and self-controlled. Be watchful. Your adversary, the devil, walks around like a roaring lion, seeking whom he may devour. (1 Peter 5:8)

The "thief" is clearly a reference to Satan. In war we expect destruction and killing to occur. Satan likes to destroy so much that his man, the Antichrist, is referred to as the "son of destruction" in the Bible (2 Thessalonians 2:3). We also discussed earlier that Satan "destroyed the world and made it into a wasteland" (Isaiah 14:17 NLT). The fallen angels corrupted all of God's creation. Humans, animals, plants. We see this manifesting again today through genetic modification. Scientists are mixing species together and producing all sorts of abominations. God intervened the last time creation became completely corrupted by sending a worldwide flood. This next time, he's going to personally return to earth, setup his kingdom, and rule forever.

Satan is out to destroy God's creation. That includes heaven and your afterlife. One of the ways Satan does this is by defiling and destroying sanctuaries, churches, and synagogues. In fact, he's done this from the beginning.

> By the multitude of your iniquities, in the unrighteousness of your commerce, you have profaned your sanctuaries. (Ezekiel 28:18)

The verse above is talking about Satan. It says he "profaned" his sanctuaries. Other words for that include *defiled* and *desecrated*. In effect, he ruined or destroyed his sanctuaries. So, what were those sanctuaries? Well, when Satan was created, we know he served God in heaven and he lived on earth. All of the angels were holy for a period of time. So, heaven and earth were both holy. Sin didn't exist until Satan decided he wanted to be God. Satan's sin defiled both places. He waged war against God and the holy angels in heaven. His sin got him kicked out of heaven because he defiled it! When God placed Adam and Eve in the garden of Eden, it was holy because they didn't know sin. Satan defiled it by deceiving Eve and getting her to sin. All of them got kicked out of the garden of Eden because they defiled it.

During the tribulation period, Satan's Antichrist is going to defile another sanctuary. The Third Temple in Israel will be built again. The Jewish people are going to be worshiping God there. The Antichrist, who will be possessed by Satan, is going to defile that temple.

> The man of sin is revealed, the son of destruction. He opposes and exalts himself against all that is called God or that is worshiped, so that he sits as God in the temple of God, setting himself up as God. (2 Thessalonians 2:3-4)

The Antichrist will declare himself God inside the Third Temple and demand everyone worship him. Satan destroys sanctuaries. He does this because he doesn't want us worshiping God. He wants to be worshiped instead. Another reason he attacks temples is because the Bible tells us they are replicas of the ones in heaven. In this Scripture, the "high priest" is Jesus.

> We have such a high priest, who sat down on the right hand of the throne of the Majesty in the heavens, a servant of the sanctuary and of the true tabernacle which the Lord pitched, not man. ... For if he were on earth, he would not be a priest at all, seeing there are priests who offer the gifts according to the law, who serve a copy and shadow of the heavenly things, even as Moses was warned by God when he was about to make the tabernacle, for he said, "See, you shall make everything according to the pattern that was shown to you on the mountain." (Hebrews 8:1-2, 4-5)

Moses built the first tabernacle for God on earth. God told Moses to follow his instructions for building it because it was "a copy and shadow of the heavenly" one. When Satan assaults sanctuaries, he's assaulting heaven. I think this is why Jesus was particularly angry with the merchants and money changers who were defiling the temple. You may recall that he made a whip and drove them out (John 2:14-16). They were doing commerce in God's house. Commerce was one of Satan's sins. We see this defilement in the world prominently today, don't we? Every time a church is lit on fire, crosses on the tops of Christian churches are forcibly taken down, or someone shoots people with a gun inside a synagogue.

You know there's another type of temple that Satan assaults that has everything to do with his assault on the afterlife.

> You are coming to Christ, who is the living cornerstone of God's temple. He was rejected by people, but he was chosen by God for great honor. And you are living stones that God is building into his spiritual temple. What's more, you are his holy priests. Through the mediation of Jesus Christ, you offer spiritual sacrifices that please God. (1 Peter 2:4-5 NLT)

If you have placed your faith in Jesus, then you are part of God's "spiritual temple." Do you know Satan's favorite war tactic against your holy temple? It's any sin that defiles your body. Sexual sin in particular (1 Corinthians 6:18-20). That's why the Bible calls us to live in a manner that's holy, because our bodies contain the Holy Spirit. We're dwelling places for God. Heaven is anywhere that God dwells. You know, I hadn't really thought of my body as a type of heaven until I wrote this paragraph. It's something God revealed to me in the moment. It's a bit overwhelming to think about, isn't it? When we think of ourselves like this, it becomes clear why God wants us to be pure. It's also why Satan attacks us, because he's assaulting heaven.

This leads me to one of Satan's weapons that can be quite effective against us. It's temptation. Satan is the ultimate tempter. He even tempted Jesus for 40 days in the wilderness. Remember, the Bible tells us that God doesn't ever tempt anyone (James 1:13). It all comes from Satan. Satan tempts us to defile our bodies, kill our faith, and destroy our moral behavior. He tempts us to sin. Sin pulls us away from God. God is perfect and holy. Sin is the complete opposite of that. Satan wants people to live a life of sin so that they'll never know Jesus and be saved. If we're already saved, Satan knows that if he can get us to sin, that he can draw us away from God and toward himself. We would lose all the promises of God, like everlasting life in heaven, if we abandon our faith in Jesus. We would lose rewards and treasure in heaven if we live a life of sin and unfruitfulness even though we're saved. That's his goal, to steal our promises and destroy our afterlife.

Speaking of stealing, I'm not sure we give much thought to stealing in warfare, but it's a primary tactic of Satan's. If he can't tempt us into doing what he wants, he'll just steal something from us instead. Or at least he'll try to. The main thing Satan wants to steal from you is your soul! He doesn't want you to inherit heaven and everlasting life in the holy place he wants to reign over. He wants you to be condemned to life in hell, just like him.

I'm going to be completely honest with you right now. If you aren't saved, you're opening yourself up for demonic possession. No joke! Lots of people in the Bible were possessed by demons. It's one of the main afflictions that Jesus and his disciples healed (Matthew 4:24, Acts 5:16). It didn't magically stop happening after Jesus's crucifixion. It's still prevalent today. It's obvious when we see people commit crimes that are so horrendous that only the devil or his minions could be behind it.

Another thing Satan steals is God's worship. This is where Satan reveals he is truly the master of thieves. He assaults heaven because he wants to be God and be worshiped. He's managed to convince most people who have ever lived, and even live today, to worship him already! I know you probably just said, "What?!" It's true. If you aren't worshiping Jesus, then you're probably worshiping Satan.

> By this you know the Spirit of God: every spirit who confesses that Jesus Christ has come in the flesh is of God, and every spirit who doesn't confess that Jesus Christ has come in the flesh is not of God; and this is the spirit of the Antichrist, of whom you have heard that it comes. Now it is in the world already. (1 John 4:2-3)

> Therefore, my beloved, flee from idolatry. ... What am I saying then? That a thing sacrificed to idols is anything, or that an idol is anything? But I say that the things which the Gentiles sacrifice, they sacrifice to demons and not to God, and I don't desire that you would have fellowship with demons. (1 Corinthians 10:14, 19-20)

Recall that the spirit of the Antichrist is Satan (Revelation 13). Think of all the religions on the planet who worship "God." Unless that God is Jesus Christ in the flesh, it's not the God of the Bible. If it's not the God of the Bible, then it's an idol. Idolatry is when you worship someone or something other than God. It's the first command of the Ten Commandments (Exodus 20:3-6). The apostle Paul makes it clear in the second Scripture above what idolatry really is. It's the worship of demons. That means you're really serving and praising Satan since he's the prince of demons (Matthew 12:24). No wonder God expressly forbids it. He's protecting us from our enemy Satan!

Now, if Satan can't convince you to worship him through a false god, then he'll get you to worship other things God created. God warned us against worshiping ancestors, admired people, ourselves, animals, and the heavens.

> Lest you corrupt yourselves, and make yourself a carved image in the form of any figure, the likeness of male or female, the likeness of any animal that is on the earth, the likeness of any winged bird that flies in the sky, the likeness of anything that creeps on the ground, the likeness of any fish that is in the water under the earth; and lest you lift up your eyes to the sky, and when you see the sun and the moon and the stars, even all the army of the sky, you are drawn away and worship them, and

> serve them. (Deuteronomy 4:16-19)

> Professing themselves to be wise, they became fools, and traded the glory of the incorruptible God for the likeness of an image of corruptible man, and of birds, four-footed animals, and creeping things. ... Who exchanged the truth of God for a lie, and worshiped and served the creature rather than the Creator. (Romans 1:22-23, 25)

Satan tempts us into worshiping and serving "the creature rather than the Creator." The devil is stealing worship that God deserves.

Now that you understand Satan's warfare tactics in stealing, killing, and destroying your afterlife, let's discuss how we are to engage in this war and combat his tactics. There's a component in the armor of God that is especially helpful here. It's the breastplate of righteousness. We're all sinners. None of us are righteous. Jesus is the one who makes us righteous. We effectively get this breastplate when we believe that Jesus is God in the flesh, that he died for our sins, and that he rose from the dead. We get it when we place our faith in Jesus. Once you've put your faith in Jesus, you are sealed with God's Holy Spirit (Ephesians 1:13-14). That means Satan won't be able to steal your soul! The apostle Paul confirms this with these comforting words.

> For I am persuaded that neither death, nor life, nor angels, nor principalities, nor things present, nor things to come, nor powers, nor height, nor depth, nor any other created thing will be able to separate us from God's love which is in Christ Jesus our Lord. (Romans 8:38-39)

This breastplate also helps us not give in to Satan's temptations. With the Holy Spirit living inside of us, God is destroying our sinful nature and encouraging us to behave righteously. Jesus himself preached the message of repentance and turning away from sin. That's because it goes hand in hand with our afterlife. Turning away from worldly desires helps us focus on our eternal promises. We're to keep our eyes fixed on Jesus, on heaven. In fact, we're even told to store our treasures in heaven, not on earth, so that the thief (you know, Satan) can't steal it (Matthew 6:19-20).

If you've put your faith in Jesus and you've got your breastplate of righteousness on, then don't be intimidated by your enemy. You no longer have a spirit of fear. You have the Spirit of power living inside of you (2 Timothy 1:7).

3.2. SATAN ACCUSES

The next tactic of Satan's that we need to address is accusation. Satan is our accuser.

> The great dragon was thrown down, the old serpent, he who is called the devil and Satan .... He was thrown down to the earth, and his angels were thrown down with him. I heard a loud voice in heaven, saying, "... the accuser of our brothers has been thrown down, who accuses them before our God day and night." (Revelation 12:9-10)

Here, we learn that he accuses us before God day and night. He's absolutely relentless in his accusations against us. If you think back to the garden of Eden, you'll recall that Satan first accused God. He asked Eve, "Did God really say?" (Genesis 3:1). He accused God of lying to Eve. Lying about what knowledge the fruit would give her and lying about the consequences of eating the fruit.

Let's look at a real example of this that took place in heaven before God. In this Scripture, "Yahweh" is God.

> Now on the day when God's sons came to present themselves before Yahweh, Satan also came among them. Yahweh said to Satan, "Where have you come from?" Then Satan answered Yahweh, and said, "From going back and forth in the earth, and from walking up and down in it." Yahweh said to Satan, "Have you considered my servant, Job? For there is no one like him in the earth, a blameless and an upright man, one who fears God, and turns away from evil." Then Satan answered Yahweh, and said, "Does Job fear God for nothing? Haven't you made a hedge around him, and around his house, and around all that he has, on every side? You have blessed the work of his hands, and his substance is increased in the land. But stretch out your hand now, and touch all that he has, and he will renounce you to your face." (Job 1:6-11)

Satan accused Job of worshiping God only because of all the good things God did for him. He accused Job of having a fake faith. He believed that Job would curse God if the blessings stopped and horrible things happened to him. This is what he says to God about us too you know. He wants us to renounce God.

For Job, Satan did his worst. He stole all of his livestock. He murdered all of his children. Satan removed the things God blessed Job with. Job is an absolute hero! He didn't fall for Satan's tactics. Job didn't sin by blaming God (Job 1:22). Job "maintained his integrity" even though Satan wanted him to be ruined (Job 2:3).

Now, here's a hard truth to understand. God let Satan test Job against his accusation. But Satan had some boundaries. He wasn't allowed to harm Job physically. Yikes! That means we're getting tested too. I take comfort in knowing Satan has limits and God doesn't test us beyond what we can handle (1 Corinthians 10:13). God allows this testing because it refines our faith. It makes us steadfast and immovable (James 1:3). We're able to stand against what comes our way. And when all the testing is done, we'll come out like refined gold (Job 23:10). You might even be rewarded in heaven with the crown of life (James 1:12) which is promised to those who love God and who remain steadfast under trial. Don't let Satan steal your crown.

I told you Satan was relentless. So, when Job didn't behave the way Satan desired, he went right back to accusing him again.

> Again, on the day when God's sons came to present themselves before Yahweh, Satan came also among them to present himself before Yahweh. Yahweh said to Satan, "Where have you come from?" Satan answered Yahweh, and said, "From going back and forth in the earth, and from walking up and down in it." Yahweh said to Satan, "Have you considered my servant Job? For there is no one like him in the earth, a blameless and an upright man, one who fears God, and turns away from evil. He still maintains his integrity, although you incited me against him, to ruin him without cause." Satan answered Yahweh, and said, "Skin for skin. Yes, all that a man has he will give for his life. But stretch out your hand now, and touch his bone and his flesh, and he will renounce you to your face." (Job 2:1-5)

This time Satan accused Job of only worshiping God because he still had his health. He believed that Job would curse God and essentially spit in God's face if he became ill. Once again, Satan had limits. He couldn't kill Job. Satan did his worst, yet again. Job was covered in boils from head to foot. This time even Job's wife wanted him to curse God and die. Yet Job refused to succumb to Satan's weapon! Job said nothing wrong against God.

Satan is so good at accusing us that he doesn't even have to be the one to do it all the time. He's managed to infect our culture and beliefs in such a cunning way that we accuse ourselves and each other. When Job lost everything, including his health, several friends of his arrived to comfort him. Except they weren't very comforting. They all believed Job must be some horrible sinner in order for God to afflict him so much. They became relentless in accusing him instead of Satan. They pleaded with him to repent of his sins so that God would relent.

This reveals another reason Satan accuses us. He wants us to believe we're wretched sinners who can't be saved and who don't deserve to live in heaven. None of them could fathom that what happened to Job was a test, allowed by God, delivered by Satan.

This has manifested as a major assault on the afterlife. Satan accuses us of not being good enough, that we have to earn our way into heaven. He accuses God of lying to us about heaven and hell, what heaven is like, and how to be saved. Once we place our faith in Jesus, he continues to accuse us so that we'll doubt that we really are saved. Satan knows that a doubting Christian is an ineffective, "unstable" one.

> Count it all joy, my brothers, when you fall into various temptations, knowing that the testing of your faith produces endurance. Let endurance have its perfect work, that you may be perfect and complete, lacking in nothing. But if any of you lacks wisdom, let him ask of God, who gives to all liberally and without reproach, and it will be given to him. But let him ask in faith, without any doubting, for he who doubts is like a wave of the sea, driven by the wind and tossed. For that man shouldn't think that he will receive anything from the Lord. He is a double-minded man, unstable in all his ways. (James 1:2-8)

So how do we stand against Satan's accusations? There are two components in the armor of God that are useful in this fight. The first is the helmet of salvation. If you have placed your faith in Jesus, then you must be fully confident in your salvation. You cannot doubt this! Remember that your salvation has nothing to do with you, your skills, your ability, or your wisdom. It has to do with what Jesus did <u>for</u> you.

Trust that God is good enough, not yourself.

The next is the shield of faith. Faith deflects Satan's arrows of accusation. Faith conquers doubt. To use this shield, you need to be able to recall the Word of God. Think about God's promises to you and how he's been faithful to you.

The most important weapon against Satan's accusations is your advocate. Job knew this too.

> Even now my witness is in heaven. My advocate is there on high. (Job 16:19 NLT)

This advocate is Jesus Christ.

> My dear children, I am writing this to you so that you will not sin. But if anyone does sin, we have an advocate who pleads our case before the Father. He is Jesus Christ, the one who is truly righteous. (1 John 2:1 NLT)

When we place our faith in Jesus, we're sealed with the Holy Spirit, who is also described as the Advocate (John 14:26). That's because it's Jesus's Spirit living inside of us. He gives us peace of mind (John 14:27). When Satan's accusations come against you, and they will, remember that no one can bring a "charge against God's chosen ones." Jesus is there to tell Satan that we're not condemned. He saved us!

> There is therefore now no condemnation to those who are in Christ Jesus, who don't walk according to the flesh, but according to the Spirit. ... Who could bring a charge against God's chosen ones? It is God who justifies. Who is he who condemns? It is Christ who died, yes rather, who was raised from the dead, who is at the right hand of God, who also makes intercession for us. (Romans 8:1, 33-34)

3.3. SATAN DECEIVES

The last warfare tactic of Satan's that we're going to examine is deception.

> The great dragon was thrown down, the old serpent, he who is called the devil and Satan, the deceiver of the whole world. (Revelation 12:9)

Satan is called the "deceiver of the whole world." It means to cause to go astray, to lead someone away from the truth. Satan wants you to believe things that aren't true. Jesus refers to him as the father of lies (John 8:44). I really think this is Satan's go-to weapon. Satan had to have started his war in heaven with a giant deception. How else could he convince a third of the angels to follow him? He must have deceived them about his own might and about God being weak. Then he started his war against our afterlife with another deception. In the garden of Eden, Eve was deceived. Satan flat out lied to her when he told her she wouldn't die.

If Satan can convince the world that he doesn't exist, that God isn't real, that heaven and hell are something other than what the Bible says, that humanity is doomed because of climate change or a rogue asteroid, then what will people do? They certainly won't give God any glory. Instead, they'll replace God with anyone and anything else that they believe will save them.

Let's look at some specific ways that Satan deceives us. A big one is false teachers and false prophets. Jesus warned us about this.

> Jesus answered them, "Be careful that no one leads you astray. For many will come in my name, saying, 'I am the Christ,' and will lead many astray. ... Many false prophets will arise and will lead many astray. ... For false christs and false prophets will arise, and they will show great signs and wonders, so as to lead astray, if possible, even the chosen ones. Behold, I have told you beforehand." (Matthew 24:4-5, 11, 24-25)

So, what do false teachers do specifically? Well, the apostle Peter gives us a long list of their qualities in 2 Peter 2. Here are some of the things he describes. They teach destructive heresies. They deny God. Their teaching is evil. They are immoral. They slander the truth. They are greedy and just want your money. They speak evil of things they don't understand. They scoff at the supernatural. They indulge in evil pleasures and deception. They lust with their eyes. They lure people into sin. They are proud, arrogant, and brag about themselves. In fact, Peter says "their desire for sin is never satisfied" (2 Peter 2:14 NLT).

Did you know that pride is a deception (Obadiah 1:3)? Your own pride can, in fact, deceive you. It deceived Satan. He put all of his faith in himself and his ability to defeat God. We as a people group are just like him.

> But know this: that in the last days, grievous times will come. For men will be lovers of self, lovers of money, boastful, arrogant, blasphemers, disobedient to parents, unthankful, unholy. (2 Timothy 3:1-2)

People certainly love themselves. Think of all the selfies that are plastered all over the Internet. There's a very big trap by Satan down this road. If you trust in yourself, whether that's your skill, your smarts, or your wealth, then you very well might believe you don't have any need for God. That's the very sin that Jesus called out the church of Laodicea for committing (Revelation 3:17). It was Jesus's last warning to the churches. You know, Jesus's letters to the churches in the book of Revelation can be viewed as a progression of warnings through the future. Since Laodicea is the last church, it speaks to us. I am absolutely convinced that we are the last generation before Jesus returns. The signs are overwhelming. This warning is imperative for us today. We cannot be deceived by our own arrogance. We cannot become a false teacher boasting about our ability to save mankind. In Part 4 of this book, we're going to discuss many ways Satan is assaulting our afterlife by using our very own pride.

You must understand that most false teachers don't advertise themselves as such. That would be bad for business. No, they want you to believe they are peddling the truth.

> For such men are false apostles, deceitful workers, masquerading as Christ's apostles. And no wonder, for even Satan masquerades as an angel of light. It is no great thing therefore if his servants also masquerade as servants of righteousness. (2 Corinthians 11:13-15)

Satan and the false teachers who essentially work for him pretend to be Jesus's apostles, "servants of righteousness." The Bible refers to Jesus as the Word (John 1). So, it's no surprise that Satan mimics that with his own false words.

In addition to false teachers and false prophets deceiving us, another prominent way that Satan deceives us is through drugs. This deception is specifically mentioned in the book of Revelation. It's a sin that marks the end times.

> For with your sorcery all the nations were deceived. (Revelation 18:23)

> They didn't repent of their murders, their sorceries, their sexual immorality, or their thefts. (Revelation 9:21)

The word "sorceries" refers to drugs, idolatry, witchcraft, and poison. If Satan can get you into an altered state of consciousness where you aren't able to think clearly, then he knows you'll be open to his lies. We've all seen the headlines and news reports about drug addiction being an epidemic today. It's not just drugs. It's anything that alters your mind. That includes alcohol and even porn.

Another warning for us living in the end times is to be watchful of counterfeit signs, miracles, and power.

> Then the lawless one will be revealed ... even he whose coming is according to the working of Satan with all power and signs and lying wonders, and with all deception of wickedness for those who are being lost, because they didn't receive the love of the truth, that they might be saved. (2 Thessalonians 2:8-10)

The "lawless one" is referring to the Antichrist. The leader who will come to power during the tribulation period. His power will come from Satan. He's going to perform signs to deceive people into believing that he is God. Most people are going to believe him. But you don't have to. You can choose to see the truth instead of the lies. The first step in combating Satan's deception is to remove his blindfold. Yes, that's right, he's blinded everyone who hasn't put their faith in Jesus. In the first Scripture below, Satan is the "god of this world."

> Even if our Good News is veiled, it is veiled in those who are dying, in whom the god of this world has blinded the minds of the unbelieving, that the light of the Good News of the glory of Christ, who is the image of God, should not dawn on them. (2 Corinthians 4:3-4)

> But whenever someone turns to the Lord, the veil is taken away. (2 Corinthians 3:16)

All you have to do to not be deceived is "turn to the Lord." Jesus is the Lord. You just need to put your faith in him.

Now, how do you think all of this deception manifests today as an assault on the afterlife? How about the lie that there are multiple paths to God and heaven? Or that heaven is for boring losers and hell is where all the cool people are going to party it up in the afterlife. There are countless lies and deceptions about the afterlife spreading in the world and infecting people.

It's no wonder that deception abounds today because most preachers aren't teaching straight from the Bible anymore. Instead, they're preaching "feel good" sermons. They aren't equipping you to deal with the onslaught of lies. You must seek out teachers and preachers who want to educate you about God's entire truth. That means they don't skip any books or content in the Bible, like Bible prophecy or the book of Revelation. Satan is so easily able to deceive us because we don't know the truth!

Truth is your weapon in this war. Remember from the armor of God that you must wield the sword of the Spirit. And we know the Spirit is truth. The sword is a reference to the Word of God.

> For the word of God is living and active, and sharper than any two-edged sword, piercing even to the dividing of soul and spirit, of both joints and marrow, and is able to discern the thoughts and intentions of the heart. (Hebrews 4:12)

Now, in order for you to use the Word, you have to know the Word. That's where another component of the armor of God comes into play. The belt of truth. This is you knowing God's Word so well that you can bring his truths to mind when you most need to. You have to store it in your heart and be able to pull it out like a tool from a utility belt. This is why it's so important to have a good teacher and to have good study habits. Be sure you're reading your Bible every day. Look up topics in the Bible that you'd like better understanding of. Be able to spot a false teacher, like Satan.

The Bible tells us exactly how to do that, identify a deceiver. When the apostle Paul was teaching to Jewish people in Berea, they listened to what he had to say and then looked it up for themselves in the Scriptures. They wanted to make sure that what he said was legit. Furthermore, we're told to test the spirits at work in people.

> Beloved, don't believe every spirit, but test the spirits, whether they are of God, because many false prophets have gone out into the world. By this you know the Spirit of God: every spirit who confesses that Jesus Christ has come in the flesh is of God, and every spirit who doesn't confess that Jesus Christ has come in the flesh is not of God; and this is the spirit of the Antichrist, of whom you have heard that it comes. Now it is in the world already. (1 John 4:1-3)

Anyone who doesn't acknowledge and teach that Jesus is God in the flesh is in fact a false prophet. That person has the spirit of the Antichrist, which you know is Satan. Don't listen to those people!

Satan doesn't just rely on false teachers to get his message and lies into the world. He spreads it any way he can. In this next chapter coming up, I'm going to expose Satan's wartime propaganda.

CHAPTER 4 - SATAN'S WARTIME PROPAGANDA

Satan has an entire army, not of fallen angels but of captive people who spread his wartime propaganda willingly. People who aren't saved don't have the Holy Spirit living inside of them. The Holy Spirit is the Spirit of truth (John 15:26). When you don't have the truth in you, then you become someone Satan can use to spread his lies (Jude 1:19). These people are different than the false teachers and false prophets that we discussed in the last chapter. The Bible refers to these propaganda spreaders as scoffers and mockers.

> In the last days scoffers will come, mocking the truth and following their own desires. (2 Peter 3:3 NLT)

> In the last days there will be very difficult times. For people will love only themselves and their money. They will be boastful and proud, scoffing at God, disobedient to their parents, and ungrateful. They will consider nothing sacred. (2 Timothy 3:1-2 NLT)

Scoffing means to revile, blaspheme, or express contempt. *Mocking* is quite similar but involves contemptuous ridicule. The Bible actually has a lot to say about these people and what they do. The book of Jude gives us a whole bunch of detail which includes the following: they slander celestial beings, speak evil of things they don't understand, grumble and complain, boast about themselves, flatter others for their own gain, create division, and live only to satisfy their lusts. We're also told they invent evil things (Romans 1:30) and speak empty philosophies and high-sounding nonsense (Colossians 2:8 NLT).

What nonsense in particular?

> Why am I still being persecuted? If I were no longer preaching salvation through the cross of Christ, no one would be offended. (Galatians 5:11 NLT)

The apostle Paul wrote the Scripture above. He was persecuted everywhere he went. He tells us why. It's because he preached the message of salvation through Jesus. If Paul was preaching something else, no one would have been upset. You know very well that it's the same today. No one gets offended if you believe in reincarnation, worship nature, or pray to a statue. You are free to invite someone to a psychic fair, a movie mocking God, or a new age yoga class. But invite someone to a Christian Bible teaching church, hand them a gospel tract, or even wear a MAGA hat that associates you with conservative Christian beliefs, then forget it, the gloves come off per se. The empty philosophies and nonsense are anything other than biblical truth. Satan doesn't care what you believe as long as it's not Jesus. So, he's going to protect and defend everything that's a lie and attack the truth.

Satan is assaulting our afterlife by infiltrating every aspect of our culture. The debate about the afterlife is no longer confined to the church. It's out in the open, everywhere. Propaganda is one of his weapons. He uses scoffers and mockers to deliver it.

Propaganda is the act of spreading ideas, information, or rumors in order to damage an opposing cause and to support its own. Here's how britannica.com describes it: "Propaganda is the more or less systematic effort to manipulate other people's beliefs, attitudes, or actions by means of symbols (words, gestures, banners, monuments, music, clothing, insignia, hairstyles, designs on coins and postage stamps, and so forth). ... To maximize effect, they may omit or distort pertinent facts or simply lie, and they may try to divert the attention of the reactors (the people they are trying to sway) from everything but their own propaganda."[1] Britannica further reveals there are other variables that affect human behavior that go hand in hand with the propaganda. Economic and physical incentives like gifts, a raise, or love. Social pressure is the one that caught my eye. In fact, they indicate propagandists specifically target groups that will have the most influence on a person. Groups that a person trusts or is loyal to. Think churches, clubs, sports teams, companies, and employers. Satan knows that if he can get your friend, coach, boss, teacher, or favorite actor or athlete on board with his message then he's more likely to win you over as well.

There are two key areas that I'd like to focus on where Satan is pushing propaganda for his end times assault on the afterlife. The first is entertainment. Specifically, Hollywood and video games. Check out some of these headlines.

"Matthew McConaughey Dishes Dirt On Hollywood's Christian

Bigotry"[2]

"Why Is There So Much Hell In Video Games And So Little Heaven?"[3]

"*Lucifer* Smashes Netflix Ratings As Tom Ellis Series Gains Over 1 Billion Views"[4]

"'*The Good Place*' Has Created A Heaven And Hell Perfect For Our Time"[5]

Entertainment that's anti-Christian isn't new. It's been around for a long time. I think it's because it's one of Satan's favorite ways to get his message across to the masses. According to Nielson reports, television is the most used electronic medium for adults in the US. The average adult spends slightly over four hours a day watching TV.[6] That's a lot of time that Satan can use to influence our beliefs and opinions! Let's look at some of the propaganda he's delivering that mocks the afterlife.

In *The Good Place* TV show, people earn points throughout their life. If you die with enough points, you get to go to the good place. The main character was mistakenly sent to the good place and must try to hide her sinful behavior.[7] In the TV show *Lucifer*, the devil decides to leave his rulership over hell and move to Los Angeles where he runs a nightclub. He's portrayed as sexy and charming.[8] In Amazon's recent TV show, *Upload*, people buy a virtual afterlife and then upload themselves into it before their brain stops functioning.[9] In the movie *Self/less*, popular actor Ryan Reynolds plays a billionaire diagnosed with terminal cancer who saves his life by transferring his consciousness into a younger body.[10] I'm sure you've seen a *Star Wars* movie.[11] Do you think it's assaulting the afterlife? They portray people becoming one with the force when they die.[12] I bet you also remember the popular movie, *The Sixth Sense*. The main character could see and talk to dead people.[13]

Now, you might be thinking that some of those shows and movies are depicting things that are just way too out there for people to really believe. It's just science fiction you say. Well, have a look at these headlines.

"Elon Musk's Big Neuralink Paper: Should We Prepare For The Digital Afterlife?"[14]

"Deepak Chopra And Richard Branson To Live On Forever Through AI, Here's How"[15]

"Elon Musk: Humans Must Merge With Machines Or Become Irrelevant In AI Age"[16]

"Scientists Propose Surrounding The Sun With Supercomputer To Resurrect The Dead"[17]

This brings me to the other area where Satan is pushing his propaganda. It's science. In particular, what the tech billionaires are funding. It makes me think of what Romans 1:30 says, the scoffers and mockers will invent evil things. They are certainly creating technology that will steer many people away from the real truth about how to live forever. Many people who are afraid of death and the afterlife will do almost anything in order to achieve immortality. There's so much to say about this that we're going to explore how Satan is using science and technology to assault the afterlife in future chapters in this book.

Join me and continue understanding Satan's war. In Part 2 of this book, I expose new and modern ways that he's assaulting God's dwelling place, heaven.

PART 2

SATAN'S ASSAULT ON HEAVEN

CHAPTER 5 - HEAVEN IS UNDER FIRE

You now know that Satan's war against heaven started long ago. He relentlessly continues his assault today. Heaven is under constant fire from our enemy. In Revelation 13:6 we learn that the Antichrist, who has the spirit of Satan, blasphemes God's dwelling place. Heaven is where God lives and reigns. God also created heaven.

> Yahweh says, "Heaven is my throne, and the earth is my footstool. ... For my hand has made all these things, and so all these things came to be." (Isaiah 66:1-2)

So, let's examine some of the primary lies that Satan is assaulting heaven with today. He sows doubt by getting us to question if heaven really exists. He enjoys lying about what heaven is like and what we'll be doing there. A favorite tactic of Satan's is to deceive us about how to get to heaven. To combat this assault, we need to have a good understanding of the truth regarding both heaven and hell. Now, the purpose of this chapter isn't a comprehensive study on heaven. That's already been done and very well I might add. I highly recommend you read Randy Alcorn's book, *Heaven*, if you'd like to learn everything you possibly can about the afterlife.[1] I'm just going to review some key truths with you to make sure we're all on the same page.

5.1. HEAVEN ISN'T BORING AND BUREAUCRATIC

Satan's assault against heaven today begins with the Bible. Satan doesn't want you to read the Bible, so he fills the world with lies about it. He says that it's not the Word of God. That it's full of errors. That it was written by men. That some of it isn't relevant anymore. That it doesn't give many details about heaven or hell. Well, the Bible is full of information about heaven and hell. That's why Satan doesn't want you reading it. That makes sense because it's the authority on heaven and hell. It's literally God's Word. It's not like any other book. Yes, people did the actual writing of it. However, God's Holy Spirit is the one who gave the people who wrote it the actual words to write (2 Peter 1:20-21). Jesus, who you know is God in human form, referred to himself as the Word (John 1:1-18, Revelation 19:13).

God proves that we can trust the Bible by telling us what's going to happen in the future, with specific details, and then fulfilling those prophecies accurately. We can also trust that the contents of the Bible we're reading today are original and haven't been altered over time. Scripture was preserved through history by scribes. They meticulously copied the Scriptures ensuring what they recorded exactly matched the original document. If they made an error, they threw the copy away and started over. As an example, over 5,600 ancient copies of the New Testament have been found, the earliest from AD 130. Those copies are 99.5% accurate when compared to each other.[2] If you'd like to learn more about why you can trust the Bible, refer to Part 5 - Bible Basics And Glossary and Part 6 - Trusting the Bible, in my book, *Rapture 911: What To Do If You're Left Behind*.[3]

A primary lie about heaven today is that it's not real. That it doesn't exist. That heaven is just a mere happy state of being that one can achieve. In fact, it's actually become one of the definitions of the word *heaven*. Look at how Satan perpetuates this. John Lennon's immensely popular song "Imagine" has lyrics: "Imagine there's no heaven...no hell below."[4] The famous physicist, Stephen Hawking believed: 'There Is No Heaven; It's A Fairy Story.'[5] And a recent assault gaining momentum in 2021 is Robert Bigelow's contest.[6] He's the billionaire who owns Budget Suites of America and Bigelow Aerospace. He's giving away $1.5 million in a contest to whoever can prove there's an afterlife. Of course, the big problem is that using the Bible and Scripture isn't allowed. The obvious evidence of life after death is, of course, the resurrected Jesus. Here's one more example. I'm sure you've heard of Deepak Chopra, the bestselling author and one of Oprah's regular guests. Here's what he's teaching about life after death: "In the West the hereafter has been viewed as a place akin to the material world. Heaven, hell, and purgatory lie in some distant region beyond the sky or under the earth. In the India of my childhood the hereafter wasn't a place at all, but a state of awareness."[7]

You need to know that heaven is a real, physical place where real, physical things live. I think it's also good for you to understand that there are multiple places for the afterlife described in the Bible. Before you get all worked up and confused, let me explain. The garden of Eden was considered heaven. That's why Adam and Eve were kicked out after they sinned; they couldn't eat from the Tree of Life anymore (Genesis 3). It was a real place with trees, plants, animals, food, and fellowship with God. When they got kicked out, they were then subject to death. Just like we are. Before Jesus died, the Old Testament believers who died went to a place referred to as Abraham's Bosom that was deep within the earth (Luke 16:19-22). It was a place of comfort and rest. That's where Jesus went for three days when he died too (Matthew 12:40, Ephesians 4:8-10). After Jesus's resurrection, Jesus took everyone in Abraham's Bosom to the present heaven (Ephesians 4:8-10). Since Abraham's Bosom was evacuated, the only place deep within the earth is the present hell (Luke 16:19-24).

Now, don't confuse Abraham's Bosom with purgatory. That's one of Satan's lies that's completely unbiblical. There isn't a holding place where you go to be purified of sins before entering heaven. There isn't a temporary place you go where your life is evaluated and you have to defend why you should go to heaven. The popular movie *Defending Your Life* is a deception.[8] Satan desperately wants us to believe that we have to earn our way into heaven. If you've put your faith in Jesus, you must remember that there is now no more condemnation for you (Romans 8:1-4). Jesus paid your sin debt in full! When someone dies today, they immediately go to the present heaven or the present hell, depending on their relationship with Jesus.

So, anyone who has died since Jesus's resurrection goes to the present heaven to be with the Lord Jesus where he is. In the Scripture below, "the earthly house of our tent" refers to our body. We know this truth only applies to believers because they're filled with God's Spirit. The Holy Spirit is our guarantee when we put our faith in Jesus. Believers go to heaven, where Jesus currently is, when they die.

> For we know that if the earthly house of our tent is dissolved, we have a building from God, a house not made with hands, eternal, in the heavens. ... Now he who made us for this very thing is God, who also gave to us the down payment of the Spirit. ... We are courageous, I say, and are willing rather to be absent from the body and to be at home with the Lord. (2 Corinthians 5:1, 5, 8)

So where is this current heaven? We know that it's upward, in the actual heavens, in another dimension. Stephen, one of the disciples chosen after Jesus's resurrection, gazed upward and saw the heavens open and Jesus standing there (Acts 7:55-56). During the tribulation period, the sky is going to roll back and reveal what Stephen saw to all mankind (Revelation 6:14-16). People living on the earth during that time will be absolutely terrified!

Satan wants you to think that because the present heaven is in the heavens that it's an ethereal place which lacks material substance. That it's just clouds and spirit beings. Well, we have details about what the present heaven looks like. I think the most vivid depiction we have of the present heaven is the city of New Jerusalem.

> He carried me away in the Spirit to a great and high mountain, and showed me the holy city, Jerusalem, coming down out of heaven from God, having the glory of God. Her light was like a most precious stone, as if it were a jasper stone, clear as crystal; having a great and high wall; having twelve gates, and at the gates twelve angels.... ... The city is square, and its length is as great as its width. He measured the city with the reed, twelve thousand twelve stadia. ... The construction of its wall was jasper. The city was pure gold, like pure glass. The foundations of the city's wall were adorned with all kinds of precious stones. ... The twelve gates were twelve pearls. Each one of the gates was made of one pearl. The street of the city was pure gold, like transparent glass. (Revelation 21:10-12, 16, 18-19, 21)

The Bible describes the New Jerusalem as a physical place. The city is enormous, 1,400 miles wide, 1,400 miles high, and 1,400 miles long. Its wall is made of jasper and the city is made of pure gold. We're all familiar with cities. What they look like and what goes on in them. The New Jerusalem will be familiar yet wonderfully new. You know, when Moses built God's tabernacle, God gave him specific instructions to follow because it was a copy of the one in heaven (Hebrews 8:5, 9:24). We can know heaven because we know earth. Did you know that God's throne room is in this city? In these verses, God is with 24 elders who are real people wearing white with gold crowns.

> Behold, there was a throne set in heaven, and one sitting on the throne that looked like a jasper stone and a sardius. There was a rainbow around the throne, like an emerald to look at. Around the throne were twenty-

four thrones. On the thrones were twenty-four elders sitting, dressed in white garments, with crowns of gold on their heads. (Revelation 4:2-4)

And here we learn that a river comes out of God's throne and waters the Tree of Life which bears "twelve kinds of fruits." Remember the Tree of Life from the garden of Eden? Here it is in heaven.

> He showed me a river of water of life, clear as crystal, proceeding out of the throne of God and of the Lamb, in the middle of its street. On this side of the river and on that was the tree of life, bearing twelve kinds of fruits, yielding its fruit every month. The leaves of the tree were for the healing of the nations. (Revelation 22:1-2)

Also in the present heaven are animals. Jesus and the people in heaven all ride horses when they return to earth at Jesus's second coming (Revelation 19). Here's something to look forward to. If you're a believer, Jesus is making a place just for you in this heavenly city (John 14:2-3). Don't let Satan trick you into believing you don't have a real home waiting for you!

Another place described as an afterlife in the Bible is the millennial kingdom. That's when Jesus returns to earth at his second coming and reigns on earth for a literal 1,000 years. Heaven opens and Jesus, "the Lamb" and the one called "Faithful and True," returns to earth with everyone who's in the present heaven. They are referred to as "the armies," "the saints," and "the souls of those" beheaded during the tribulation period. Wherever God dwells is heaven. Since Jesus is God and he'll be on earth, that means the millennial kingdom is going to be heaven. In these verses, "his wife" refers to the church, the bride of Christ, those who've put their faith in Jesus. Those believers are wearing white linen. It's clear that the believers return to earth with Jesus since they "followed him on white horses." If you've put your faith in Jesus, then you'll be on one of those horses. That's because Jesus takes us up to heaven prior to the tribulation events. If you aren't familiar with the rapture, I discuss it more in Chapter 19.

> "For the wedding of the Lamb has come, and his wife has made herself ready." It was given to her that she would array herself in bright, pure, fine linen, for the fine linen is the righteous acts of the saints. ... I saw the

> heaven opened, and behold, a white horse, and he who sat on it is called Faithful and True. In righteousness he judges and makes war. ... He is clothed in a garment sprinkled with blood. His name is called "The Word of God." The armies which are in heaven, clothed in white, pure, fine linen, followed him on white horses. ... I saw the souls of those who had been beheaded for the testimony of Jesus and for the word of God, and such as didn't worship the beast nor his image, and didn't receive the mark on their forehead and on their hand. They lived and reigned with Christ for a thousand years. ... Blessed and holy is he who has part in the first resurrection. Over these, the second death has no power, but they will be priests of God and of Christ, and will reign with him one thousand years. (Revelation 19:7-8, 11, 13-14, 20:4, 6)

Now, it's not hard to imagine what the millennial kingdom is going to look like or be like. It's earth. We're totally familiar with it and what living here is like, aren't we? It's a real place. An important point to know is that Jesus is going to restore the earth during his reign. It appears the curse upon the earth is gradually lifted until it's completely gone at the end of Jesus's reign (Revelation 22:3).

Jesus is going to reign from Jerusalem. There won't be any more crying. Even the animals will get along. Note that "the sinner" who dies at 100 years old is cursed. That means people will live a really long time. It'll be a return to what the earth was like before the flood. Now, those people living hundreds of years are the people who place their faith in Jesus after the rapture and then survive the tribulation period. If you're a believer, you'll be there too since you come back with Jesus at his second coming. But you'll be immortal. That's pretty cool to think about!

> "But be glad and rejoice forever in that which I create; for, behold, I create Jerusalem to be a delight, and her people a joy. I will rejoice in Jerusalem, and delight in my people; and the voice of weeping and the voice of crying will be heard in her no more. No more will there be an infant who only lives a few days, nor an old man who has not filled his days; for the child will die one hundred years old, and the sinner being one hundred years old will be accursed. ... The wolf and the lamb will feed together. The lion will eat straw like the ox. Dust will be the serpent's food. They will not hurt nor destroy in all my holy mountain," says Yahweh. (Isaiah 65:18-20, 25)

Also coming into focus at Jesus's second coming is the eternal hell or lake of fire (Matthew 25:31-46). We'll review hell in more detail in the next sub chapter.

Lastly, there's the new earth and new heaven which God creates at the end of his millennial reign on earth. This is where believers will dwell for eternity.

> I saw a new heaven and a new earth, for the first heaven and the first earth have passed away, and the sea is no more. I saw the holy city, New Jerusalem, coming down out of heaven from God, prepared like a bride adorned for her husband. ... The nations will walk in its light. The kings of the earth bring the glory and honor of the nations into it. ... There will in no way enter into it anything profane, or one who causes an abomination or a lie, but only those who are written in the Lamb's book of life. (Revelation 21:1-2, 24, 27)

The eternal heaven will be the new earth that God creates after Jesus's millennial reign on earth. The city of New Jerusalem that's in the present heaven will come down to the new earth. God will make his home with us on that new earth. Now, we've already established that you know what earth is like. You know it's a physical place with nations, cities, businesses, homes, mountains, trees, animals, food, etc. The new version is going to be all that we know, but way better. God isn't going to reinvent everything that we know and love about earth. He's just going to make it brand new. The eternal heaven is absolutely a physical place.

The Scripture above states that "the kings of the earth" are in this New Jerusalem. Recall from the verses we read earlier in Revelation 19 regarding the people who return with Jesus at his second coming. They get to reign with him. If you're a believer, then that's you! If you want to be included, you can. Jesus is the gatekeeper of the pearly gates of heaven and your name must be in his "book of life." You just need to put your faith in Jesus. I tell you how in Chapter 5.3 - How To Be Saved.

Now that we've established that Satan is lying about heaven being a state of mind or just a cloud kingdom, let's consider another of his lies. Satan wants you to believe that Heaven is boring and bureaucratic. That it isn't a destination anyone would desire. That it's just plain horrible. Some popular TV shows and a recent movie are pushing this lie, including *Good Omens*, *The Good Place*, and Disney and Pixar's *Soul*.[9]

Does anything the Bible has described about heaven that we've reviewed so far come across as boring? Let's see, we get to live in a city made of pure gold and reign with Jesus. Wow, that's really going to be a bummer... Not! If you enjoy all the wonderful things God created for us on earth, you're going to be blown away by the glorious things he's created for us in heaven. Earth isn't boring, so why would heaven be boring? To think that heaven is boring is to view God himself as boring. God is the creator of everything. He never stops inventing new things. I think this is one of Satan's stupidest lies because it doesn't make any sense if you think about it. Sure, there's going to be work to do in heaven. But it's going to be fulfilling, rewarding, and will give us joy. Work won't be a burden like it is for us now. It won't be something we have to do to earn a living. It won't make us completely exhausted. God created us to do good works (Ephesians 2:10). That promise is going to be completely fulfilled for each one of us in heaven. Jesus will give us rest from our burdens (Matthew 11:28-30).

So, does that mean we're going to sit around all day singing songs to Jesus? That we're never going to have any fun? Satan certainly wants you to think that. Yes, there will be singing in heaven (Revelation 5:13). But that's not the only way to worship God. You show your reverence for God every day in how you think and behave. When you're in heaven, you're going to bring glory to God through everything you do. As for fun, just think of all the things you'll be able to do and explore in the present heaven and on the new earth. Satan's lie is that heaven can't possibly be fun because there's no fun without sin. Want to try a new sport, learn a new skill, go on an adventure to a remote island, or even talk to someone who lived centuries before you did? Go for it! I'm sure we'll even be able to explore other planets and galaxies. God wants us to enjoy all of his creation.

You know what else Satan wants you to believe about heaven? He wants you to think it's full of red tape. That there's endless layers of angel management, communication problems, and that God is aloof and not approachable. Well, in the Scriptures we read a bit earlier in this chapter you saw that believers are referred to as the wife or bride of Christ (Revelation 19:7). The apostle Paul told us that earthly marriage is an illustration of our relationship with Jesus (Ephesians 5:31-32). Marriages are intimate. They aren't bureaucratic. Husbands are told to love their wives like Jesus loves the church (Ephesians 5:25). Well, Jesus died for his church. He has a sacrificial love for us. That's not the picture of an uncaring, aloof relationship. Jesus wants us to have a personal, intimate relationship with him now, before we even get to heaven.

Now, as for red tape and obstacles in heaven. You have to remember that there's absolutely no sin in heaven. It's perfect and holy because God is perfect and holy. Red tape, obstacles, and lack of communication all imply a process that's flawed and isn't working optimally. There will be no imperfect processes in heaven! God orchestrates the tiniest of details today on earth and in heaven. Do you think he's going to just stop being in control? Think about it for a minute. Has the sun ever not risen the next morning? Job got a lesson from God about his omnipotence. God asked Job if he could direct the movement of the stars, make lightning strike, or command the morning to appear. Of course, Job couldn't. But God can and does!

There's so much more we could talk about regarding heaven. We've only scratched the surface. I'm going to expose more of Satan's lies and assaults against heaven throughout this entire book. For now, let's move on and discuss how Satan is assaulting the afterlife by lying to you about hell.

5.2. HELL ISN'T FUN AND EXCITING

Satan assaults heaven when he lies about hell. He wants to keep anyone he can from knowing the truth about heaven. He doesn't want anyone saved. His goal is to steal the promise of our afterlife in heaven away from us. He's a murderer who wants us to die the second death in the lake of fire (Revelation 20:14). So, he does everything he can to make hell appealing. He wants you to think it's the cool party place where all the popular people are going to be, where all the fun is going to take place in the afterlife, and where everything exciting is going to happen. There's a popular TV show, *Lucifer*, that has glorified Satan and proliferates many of these lies.[10]

Let's see what hell is really all about. This Scripture depicts the present hell. It's deep within the earth. Jesus is the one who told this account. Two people died, a rich man and a beggar. The rich man went to the present hell and the beggar went to Abraham's Bosom.

> "The beggar died, and he was carried away by the angels to Abraham's bosom. The rich man also died and was buried. In Hades, he lifted up his eyes, being in torment, and saw Abraham far off, and Lazarus at his bosom. He cried and said, 'Father Abraham, have mercy on me, and send Lazarus, that he may dip the tip of his finger in water and cool my tongue! For I am in anguish in this flame.' But Abraham said, 'Son, remember that you, in your lifetime, received your good things, and Lazarus, in the same way, bad things. But here he is now comforted and you are in anguish. Besides all this, between us and you there is a great gulf fixed, that those who want to pass from here to you are not able, and that no one may cross over from there to us.'" (Luke 16:22-26)

You'll notice that Abraham's Bosom, which we discussed in the prior sub chapter, was located inside the earth near the present hell. Remember that Jesus took everyone out of Abraham's Bosom at his resurrection and all those people are now in the present heaven. We learn that the rich man could see and talk to Abraham, who was in Abraham's Bosom. The rich man is in anguish because he's thirsty and he's hot because there's a flame. We also discover there's a "great gulf" between the present hell and Abraham's Bosom. No one is able to pass between the two places. Now, what part of that description is appealing, fun, or exciting? That's right. None of it is! Satan is such a liar.

You know what else Satan lies about regarding hell? He says that he's the king of hell. That he decides who goes there and that he's in charge of what happens in his kingdom. There's another place in the Bible described as the "bottomless pit." Sometimes it's confused with hell. It's different than the present or eternal hell. It's also deep within the earth. This place isn't for humans. The pit is for demons and fallen angels. In fact, some of those fallen angels are already locked up in this pit because their sin was so egregious to God (Jude 1:6). Remember from an earlier chapter that they left heaven so they could marry human women (Genesis 6:1-4).

> The demons kept begging Jesus not to send them into the bottomless pit.
> (Luke 8:31 NLT)

I want you to notice something here. Who has authority to send the demons to the pit? Jesus does. Not Satan. This will become even clearer when we look at the eternal hell. Now, if the present hell isn't bad enough, the eternal hell is far worse. Here's how it's described.

> The devil who deceived them was thrown into the lake of fire and sulfur, where the beast and the false prophet are also. They will be tormented day and night forever and ever. ... I saw the dead, the great and the small, standing before the throne, and they opened books. Another book was opened, which is the book of life. The dead were judged out of the things which were written in the books, according to their works. ... Death and Hades were thrown into the lake of fire. This is the second death, the lake of fire. If anyone was not found written in the book of life, he was cast into the lake of fire. (Revelation 20:10, 12, 14-15)

A "lake of fire and sulfur" is the second death. That sounds like volcanic lava to me, doesn't it to you? It's the place of eternal punishment (Matthew 25:46). There's something rather curious about it too though. When I think of fire, I think of light. A flame gives off a lot of light. But it doesn't in this lake of fire. In several parables, Jesus referred to the eternal hell as outer darkness (Matthew 8:12, 22:13, 25:30). A fire that doesn't provide light. The apostle Paul tells us the eternal hell is a place that's forever separated from God and his glory (2 Thessalonians 1:9). Well, God is light (John 8:12). So, it makes perfect sense that hell is the complete opposite of that.

Contrary to what Satan wants you to believe, he isn't going to be hosting a wild party in the darkness of this fiery lake. The verses above tell us that there is torment "day and night forever." There's only weeping and gnashing of teeth (Matthew 8:12). Gnashing is when you grind your teeth together. It tells us there will be immense pain and suffering in the eternal hell. Not only that, but you also read in the Scripture above that "the devil," Satan, is thrown into the lake of fire with the Antichrist, who is "the beast," and the False Prophet. In fact, God created this wretched place for Satan! The devil is certainly not the ruler of hell.

> "The eternal fire which is prepared for the devil and his angels." (Matthew 25:41)

God didn't create the lake of fire for you. He created heaven for you.

But you need to realize that heaven isn't your default destination. Of course, Satan wants you to believe that everyone goes to heaven, or at least all the good people do. And you have to be really bad, like a serial killer, to go to hell. That's so very far from the truth.

> "You can enter God's Kingdom only through the narrow gate. The highway to hell is broad, and its gate is wide for the many who choose that way. But the gateway to life is very narrow and the road is difficult, and only a few ever find it." (Matthew 7:13-14 NLT)

You have to choose to go to heaven by accepting Jesus into your life. In the next sub chapter, you'll learn how to do just that.

5.3. HOW TO BE SAVED

If you haven't placed your faith for salvation in the nail-pierced hands of Jesus Christ, then you aren't saved. You must have a personal relationship with Jesus if you want to be saved and live in heaven. I'm going to tell you how to do that. If you think of yourself as a Christian, but aren't 100% confident that you're saved, know that you can be absolutely certain! Satan's tactic in his assault on the afterlife is one of lies and doubt. He wants you to think there are multiple ways to be saved or get to heaven, and that you can't ever be certain until you get to your final destination.

God loves you and wants to spend eternity with you. But there's a problem, and it's called sin. Sin is doing and even thinking anything that isn't perfect and holy. Every single one of us commits sin. We can't help it; it's our nature. It doesn't matter what your sin is or how big or little you perceive your sin to be. It could be lying, lust, pride, or murder (Galatians 5:16-26). Any sin is sin in God's eyes.

> As it is written, "There is no one righteous; no, not one. There is no one who understands. There is no one who seeks after God. They have all turned away. They have together become unprofitable. There is no one who does good, no, not so much as one." (Romans 3:10-12)

God is perfect and sinless and righteous in every way. Thus, so is where he lives, heaven. Sin is the opposite of God. Sin cannot exist in heaven.

> For all have sinned, and fall short of the glory of God. (Romans 3:23)

Since people are inherently sinful, no one can live with God unless the sin problem is taken care of first. Sin leads to death and keeps us from the heavenly afterlife that God desires for us. Case in point: Adam and Eve. They lived in the garden of Eden with God. They saw God every day. Heaven is wherever God is, so they essentially lived in heaven. After they sinned and ate from the forbidden tree, they got kicked out of the garden. They couldn't live with God anymore. They couldn't live immortally anymore. That's why they were forbidden from eating from the Tree of Life. They were destined to die because of sin. This Scripture records that event. God sent "the man," which is Adam, and "the woman," which is Eve, out from the garden. As we've discussed earlier, "the serpent" is Satan.

> God said, "... Have you eaten from the tree that I commanded you not to eat from?" The man said, "The woman whom you gave to be with me, she gave me fruit from the tree, and I ate it." Yahweh God said to the woman, "What have you done?" The woman said, "The serpent deceived me, and I ate." ... Yahweh God said, "Behold, the man has become like one of us, knowing good and evil. Now, lest he reach out his hand, and also take of the tree of life, and eat, and live forever—" Therefore Yahweh God sent him out from the garden of Eden, to till the ground from which he was taken. So he drove out the man; and he placed cherubim at the east of the garden of Eden, and a flaming sword which turned every way, to guard the way to the tree of life. (Genesis 3:11-13, 22-24)

Here's the good news: God has a solution for the sin problem. He demands a perfect and spotless sacrifice to atone for sin. When Adam and Eve first sinned, God killed an animal to clothe them and atone for their sin (Genesis 3:21). In the Old Testament times before Jesus came, God's people sacrificed animals to atone for their sin (Leviticus 4:27-29, Hebrews 13:11). It's because the payment required for sin is death.

> For the wages of sin is death, but the free gift of God is eternal life in Christ Jesus our Lord. (Romans 6:23)

Now, don't run off to find an animal you can sacrifice to atone for your sin. God's already taken care of the sacrifice offering permanently for you. He loves you so much that he sent Jesus, his perfect and sinless and righteous son, down to earth to live as a man. Jesus was then sacrificed for you (John 19). He was crucified to atone for your sin. That's right, Jesus died for you long ago, before you ever came to faith in him. While you were still a sinner.

> But God commends his own love toward us, in that while we were yet sinners, Christ died for us. (Romans 5:8)

We know this worked because Jesus isn't dead! God raised him from the dead.

> Now after the Sabbath, as it began to dawn on the first day of the week, Mary Magdalene and the other Mary came to see the tomb. Behold, there was a great earthquake, for an angel of the Lord descended from the sky and came and rolled away the stone from the door and sat on it. His appearance was like lightning, and his clothing white as snow. For fear of him, the guards shook, and became like dead men. The angel answered the women, "Don't be afraid, for I know that you seek Jesus, who has been crucified. He is not here, for he has risen, just like he said. Come, see the place where the Lord was lying. Go quickly and tell his disciples." ... As they went to tell his disciples, behold, Jesus met them, saying, "Rejoice!" (Matthew 28:1-7, 9)

Then Jesus appeared to hundreds of people in his risen state (1 Corinthians 15:3-8). All you have to do now is believe.

> If you will confess with your mouth that Jesus is Lord and believe in your heart that God raised him from the dead, you will be saved. (Romans 10:9)

Belief. It seems too simple, doesn't it? But that's the irony of it. It's not simple at all. In fact, belief is really hard. The Bible says the path to God is narrow and most don't find it. That's because we're accustomed to striving for what we want down here on earth. The harder we work, the more we get. We love to boast about our accomplishments. We love to be in control. We want to earn our way into heaven and it's one of Satan's go-to lies. That's not God's way. God is in control, and it's about what God did, not what you've done. His solution is a gift. He gave his son as a gift to you. You just have to accept it. Being "dead through trespasses" means we were condemned to death because of our sin.

> But God, being rich in mercy, for his great love with which he loved us, even when we were dead through our trespasses, made us alive together with Christ—... for by grace you have been saved through faith, and that not of yourselves; it is the gift of God, not of works, that no one would boast. (Ephesians 2:4-5, 8-9)

Perhaps you believe Satan's lie that you don't deserve to go to heaven. That you're a bad person and committed sins that can't be forgiven. That's where grace comes in. You see, it's God's grace that saved you. As sinners, we are doomed to an eternal life far removed from God. That's God's rule. Grace is God demonstrating his love for us by pardoning us based on us believing Jesus died for our sins. God treated Jesus the way we deserve to be treated. Jesus was crucified. We deserve to be crucified for our sins against God. Jesus took that punishment. It doesn't matter what you've done. No sin is too big for Jesus to absolve! God did that so that he could treat you the way that Jesus deserves to be treated. Jesus is now in heaven with God. God wants you in heaven with him too.

A person who believes what they cannot yet see has faith. They believe God and that Jesus died for their sins. Have faith.

> Now faith is assurance of things hoped for, proof of things not seen. (Hebrews 11:1)

Here's what you must come to believe:

> You recognize that you are a sinner.
> You don't want to be a sinner anymore. You ask God to forgive you.
> You want to live with God for eternity in heaven.
> You know that you can't save yourself or earn your way into heaven.
> You believe that God sent his son Jesus to atone for your sin by dying on the cross.

You believe that God raised Jesus from the dead and that Jesus reigns with God in heaven.
You surrender your salvation to Jesus and ask him to come into your life.

Now, you can't just go through the motions and say these things. You have to actually mean them, deep down, from your heart. That's what faith is all about.

This is the good news of the Bible. That Jesus, God in the flesh, died for your sins, rose from the grave, and reigns from heaven.

> Now I declare to you, brothers, the Good News which I preached to you, which also you received, in which you also stand, by which also you are saved, if you hold firmly the word which I preached to you—unless you believed in vain. For I delivered to you first of all that which I also received: that Christ died for our sins according to the Scriptures, that he was buried, that he was raised on the third day according to the Scriptures. (1 Corinthians 15:1-4)

If you truly believe all those things, then tell God. That's what praying is, just talking to God. Tell him you believe each of those truths and ask him to come into your life. And he will indeed!

Here's an example prayer you can say to God:

"Lord Jesus, I know that I'm a sinner and that I need your forgiveness so that I can live with you for eternity in heaven. Please forgive me. I believe that you are the son of God, God in the flesh, and that you died on the cross for my sins. I believe that you alone have the power of life and death and thus you rose from the grave! I want to turn from my sins and trust and follow you as Lord and Savior. Please come into my heart and life. In Jesus's name, amen."

Now be confident that you are truly saved! You are sealed with God's Holy Spirit as a guarantee of your salvation (Ephesians 1:13-14). Nothing, not even Satan himself, can steal you from Jesus.

> Jesus answered them, "... I give eternal life to them. They will never perish, and no one will snatch them out of my hand. My Father who has given them to me is greater than all. No one is able to snatch them out of my Father's hand. I and the Father are one." (John 10:25, 28-30)

CHAPTER 6 - BURNING MAN

If you've never been to a burning man event, I'm sure you've seen footage of one on the news. At these events a giant effigy, usually of a man, is set on fire. There are many of these events in the United States and even around the globe. The most popular one is Burning Man and it's held in Black Rock City, Nevada each year.[1] Israel has an event they call Midburn that's very similar to the one in Nevada.[2] There's even one in my home state of NM that's called Zozobra.[3]

Let's reveal what takes place at Burning Man in Nevada. The event takes place on the playa, a dry lake, of the Black Rock Desert. It's held annually at the end of August, beginning of September for about 10 days. It culminates on the Saturday before Labor Day. Burning Man started in Nevada in 1991 with 600 attendees. It's grown considerably since then. In 2019, there were nearly 80,000 people there to watch the burn. The temporary Black Rock City, created by participants, literally springs up in the desert to support all the people. In 2020 the event was held in a virtual reality environment due to Covid and had over 500,000 attendees.

There are two key burns at the event. A wooden effigy of a man is burned and so is a wooden temple. The man has gotten taller over the years. It started out at 40 feet tall in 1991. It was 105 feet tall in 2017. In 2020 and 2021 the event was held in a virtual reality environment due to Covid. This enabled the man to be infinitely tall.[4] They refer to the temple as the soul of Burning Man.[5] During the week, participants can place offerings in the temple. Many people write letters to deceased loved ones or themselves. The temple for 2021 is a giant lotus flower. The man and the temple are burned at the end of the event as acts of release, cleansing, and healing.

As for what takes place during the week, I like how Carl Teichrib describes it in his book, *Game of Gods*: "Describing Burn Man is notoriously difficult. Is it a festival? Is the Burn an experiment in social cohesion, or a model of libertarianism? Is it about art and play? Is it hedonism, nudity and debauchery, or introspection and spirituality? Yes and no, all at the same time. One contributor to BRC's newspaper expressed it this way, It is our palette and canvas, to create the world we can't enjoy at home... It's pagan. It's anti-religious. It's a Trojan horse... It's a chance to get out of town and hang with some good chaps. It's sex and drugs and trance music. It's artistic expression. It's a week of survival on chips-and-salsa... It's Utopia-On-A-Stick."[6]

I think you've got the idea that this is an "anything goes" type of event. Black Rock City likely surpasses Las Vegas as sin city during the week it exists. It should be obvious that it's anti-Christian.

So, what does Burning Man have to do with Satan's assault on the afterlife? I'm so glad you asked. The first thing that struck me when I read Carl's description of Burning Man is the word *utopia*. In doing my own research on the event, I found many people refer to the city that's constructed and how it operates as utopian to them. They view it as a heaven on earth. It's man's attempt to build heaven. That's how it's assaulting the afterlife. Unfortunately, their view of heaven has some serious flaws that prevent people from understanding the real heaven. This is a crafty trick by Satan. He wants you to believe that heaven is anything you want it to be. That anything goes in heaven. That there are multiple ways to heaven. It's his lie about hell being the fun party place that everyone wants to go to. Heaven is not synonymous with sin! There is no sin in heaven. It's perfect and holy because it's God's home and he is perfect and holy (Isaiah 57:15). Living a life of unrepentant sin will, in fact, keep you out of God's heaven.

Jesus instructs us believers to:

> Pray like this: "Our Father in heaven, may your name be kept holy. Let your Kingdom come. Let your will be done on earth as it is in heaven." (Matthew 6:9-10)

This does not mean we're to construct a man-made heaven on the earth. We're sinful. Any version of heaven we create is going to be an assault on the real thing. It says we're to let God's kingdom come. That's when heaven comes to earth. We can't make the earth heaven. Only Jesus can.

This whole thing reminds me of the Tower of Babel.

> The whole earth was of one language and of one speech. ... They said, "Come, let's build ourselves a city, and a tower whose top reaches to the sky, and let's make a name for ourselves, lest we be scattered abroad on the surface of the whole earth." (Genesis 11:1, 4)

This happened shortly after the flood. When Noah and his sons got off the ark, God told them to fill the earth (Genesis 9:1). He wanted them to spread out. Instead, what did they do? They got together and built a big city with a really tall tower. The *Ancient Book of Jubilees* tells us the tower was 5,433 cubits tall or 1.54 miles![7] The tallest building in the world today is the Burj Khalifa at 2,717 feet.[8] That's only half a mile. The Tower of Babel was three times higher. There's another ancient book that's not included in the Bible that gives a few more specifics about the Tower of Babel. It's the *Ancient Book of Jasher*. It is a book that's referenced in the Bible. Now, we shouldn't take it as authoritative like Scripture but should view it more like something an ancient historian wrote. Here's an excerpt:[9]

> "And the building of the tower was unto them a transgression and a sin, and they began to build it, and whilst they were building against the Lord God of heaven, they imagined in their hearts to war against him and to ascend into heaven." (Ancient Book of Jasher, chapter 9:25)

They built a city in order to assault heaven! That's exactly what's happening in the Nevada desert each year.

Burning Man has their tower too. I mentioned earlier that the man has grown taller over the years, reaching a height of 105 feet. But now in the virtual reality environment, its height is limitless. Sound familiar?

Now, let's talk about what they do to the man and the tower. I want you to think about a prominent way fire is mentioned in the Bible. What comes to mind? Sacrifice comes to my mind. Burnt offerings for God. He instituted a whole system for sacrifices in the Old Testament that the Israelites performed to cleanse themselves of their sin. They had to do that under the old system of the law to make themselves right with God. It was so they could ultimately access heaven. Their sacrifice was a form of worship to God. In the Scripture below, "Yahweh" is God.

> Yahweh had made a covenant and commanded them, saying, "You shall not fear other gods, nor bow yourselves to them, nor serve them, nor sacrifice to them; but you shall fear Yahweh, who brought you up out of the land of Egypt with great power and with an outstretched arm, and you

shall bow yourselves to him, and you shall sacrifice to him." (2 Kings 17:35-36)

There's sacrifice and worship at Burning Man too. What do you think they're worshiping? I think it's sin. And you know who the authority on sin is - Satan!

> But I say that the things which the Gentiles sacrifice, they sacrifice to demons and not to God, and I don't desire that you would have fellowship with demons. (1 Corinthians 10:20)

"Gentiles" is a term for anyone who wasn't Jewish. In the context above, it's referring to unbelievers. The apostle Paul tells us that their sacrifices are all being offered up to demons. That's what's happening at Burning Man. It's a gathering to worship and sacrifice to Satan and his fallen angels. It's an assault on heaven because God is the one deserving of worship.

I hope you noticed the symbolism of the event. It is intense. A figure of a man is set on fire. The Bible says mankind is meant to be the temple of the living God, a place for God's Spirit to dwell (2 Corinthians 6:16). Satan wants all mankind to burn in the flames of hell. Participants at the event cheer at the fall of the man. The fall of man; the Bible tells us that was caused by Satan deceiving Eve and then by Adam sinning against God's one command (Genesis 3). Satan laughs and cheers at how easy it is to lead us astray. The people are cheering at our fall, our sin. In fact, that seems to be the entire purpose of the event. A week to celebrate sin. Then a figure of a temple is set on fire. Who is it that desecrates temples (Ezekiel 28:18)? It's Satan! These two burns are indeed assaults on the afterlife.

Another problem with Burning Man is that it hasn't stayed in the desert. Its culture of "create heaven here by doing anything you want" went home with everyone. It has infected society. Consider the autonomous zones that are being setup in cities and the out-of-control riots with buildings and cars set on fire. I can see a lot of similarities to Burning Man. God doesn't want worship and sacrifices like this from us. If you want to enter heaven, you have to sacrifice your sin. You have to give it up, repent of it, and consider it nailed to the cross with Jesus. Don't let the culture of Burning Man and what goes on at these events influence you and infect your life.

> The old system under the law of Moses was only a shadow, a dim preview of the good things to come, not the good things themselves. The sacrifices under that system were repeated again and again, year after year, but they were never able to provide perfect cleansing for those who came to worship. ... For God's will was for us to be made holy by the sacrifice of the body of Jesus Christ, once for all time. ... And when sins have been forgiven, there is no need to offer any more sacrifices. And so, dear brothers and sisters, we can boldly enter heaven's Most Holy Place because of the blood of Jesus. ... Dear friends, if we deliberately continue sinning after we have received knowledge of the truth, there is no longer any sacrifice that will cover these sins. (Hebrews 10:1, 10, 18-19, 26 NLT)

Burning an effigy of a man or a temple will not provide the perfect cleansing necessary to enter heaven. Only Jesus can do that. Leave the fake utopia and idolatry of Burning Man in the dust of the desert where the serpent dwells. Put your faith in Jesus. Then offer him the sacrifices he truly desires.

> "For I desire mercy, and not sacrifice; and the knowledge of God more than burnt offerings." (Hosea 6:6)

> Present your bodies a living sacrifice, holy, acceptable to God, which is your spiritual service. (Romans 12:1)

CHAPTER 7 - BATTLE OF THE GREAT RESET

Unless you've been hiding under a rock recently and didn't take your smart phone with you, then you've heard of the Great Reset.[1] It's all over the news these days. The United Nations and the World Economic Forum have had a plan for radically changing life on the planet for years. However, it was Covid that enabled this plan to leap forward. Here's a picture from the weforum.org website that sums up the plan in just three words.[2]

"Reset the world." That's what the Great Reset is all about. So, what is it that they want to reset? They want governments and companies to invest in "green" initiatives, like the Green New Deal. They believe the planet is doomed because of us humans. They say we're causing climate change or global warming. They also want the economy to be more fair and equitable, to reset capitalism. They favor a socialist economy in which there's wealth distribution and no property ownership. Where all products become services. It would be an economy of renters. To do these things they promote what they're calling the Fourth Industrial Revolution. Enter the tech billionaires.

There are innovations happening in every industry today because of advanced technology. Solar power, self-driving cars, nano tech medicine, the space race to colonize Mars, genetic modification, CRISPR, ... I could go on and on. Now, technology isn't inherently bad. It's what we do with it. In order to effectively manage and control every aspect of nature and every human, there must be tech to inventory it and manage it. Sensors, cameras, and tracking devices need to be on and in everything. Those sensors need to be connected to the Internet so they can transfer data. Did someone say 5G? You've heard of the Internet-of-Things (IOT). With the enormous volume of data to process, Artificial Intelligence (AI) will be used to make sense of it all. You must realize that you are considered a "thing" in this Great Reset. You are both a resource and a consumer who needs to be managed and controlled.

Just like in the chapter on Burning Man, I'm sure you're starting to wonder again what this has to do with the afterlife. There are two aspects to the Great Reset that are clear assaults on heaven. The first is the "green" agenda. It's mankind shaping the earth into heaven. Satan's underlying lie is that there is no God, no heaven, and no hell. There's only us and our own ingenuity. The second aspect is about the economic reset. It's a direct attack by Satan on how heaven operates, heaven's economy. This Great Reset is one of Satan's assaults on the afterlife. As you're reading through this book, I hope you're starting to see that Satan's weapons in this war often don't look like weapons at all. He's the master of Trojan horses.

Let's start by exposing Satan's "green" weapon against heaven. It starts with the lie that God doesn't exist. That means God isn't in control of the earth or anything in creation. No one is. So that means we must control it ourselves. And the reason we must control it is because nature seems completely out of control to us. There are more earthquakes, stronger hurricanes, widespread droughts, flash floods, large forest fires, dormant volcanoes erupting, air pollution, thinning ozone layers, polar ice caps melting.... You get the picture. Satan has convinced us to worship the planet and then scientists and tech billionaires because they're going to be the ones who save us.

We must always remember that God made everything and he's in perfect control of all elements in creation.

> The everlasting God, Yahweh, the Creator of the ends of the earth, doesn't

faint. He isn't weary. His understanding is unsearchable. (Isaiah 40:28)

That Scripture says God's "understanding is unsearchable." Today, in the Internet age, we search for the answers to everything. Now, imagine your frustration if every time you searched for something you got an error that said, "infinite results, try again." That's what it'd be like to search God's knowledge. Nature hasn't gotten out of control because God doesn't know how to fix it or because he needed a break. And Jesus, God in human form, commanded the wind and the waves, elements of nature, and they immediately obeyed him (Matthew 8:23-27). The earth isn't messed up because Jesus isn't in control. So, what's really going on?

It's called the curse. Before Adam and Eve sinned, they lived in heaven. An absolute paradise. The weather and nature were perfect. When they sinned, God kicked them out of paradise and cursed all of creation (Genesis 3:17-18). Sin impacted everything.

> Against its will, all creation was subjected to God's curse. But with eager hope, the creation looks forward to the day when it will join God's children in glorious freedom from death and decay. For we know that all creation has been groaning as in the pains of childbirth right up to the present time. (Romans 8:20-22 NLT)

We cannot reverse what God has cursed. It's all connected and tied to God's plan of redemption. The earth is going to be renewed. Now, this doesn't mean it's okay to be a terrible steward of the planet. God put Adam in the garden of Eden to "cultivate and keep it" (Genesis 2:15). But there's a big difference between respecting a resource God has given us and flat out worshiping it.

Satan is trying very hard to convince the world that there's no planet B. Well, there kinda is. God calls it the new earth.

> "For, behold, I create new heavens and a new earth; and the former things will not be remembered, nor come into mind." (Isaiah 65:17)

The new earth is going to be so wonderful that we won't even think about or remember what the current earth was like. Now, that's hard to imagine, isn't it? We talked about it in Chapter 5 and learned that the city of New Jerusalem that's currently in heaven comes down to the new earth (Revelation 21-22). That city has streets of gold and the Tree of Life! And even before the new earth, Jesus is going to restore the current earth during his millennial reign. In these verses, the prophet Isaiah is telling us what happens at the second coming, when Jesus returns to Jerusalem.

> In Jerusalem, the LORD of Heaven's Armies will spread a wonderful feast for all the people of the world. It will be a delicious banquet with clear, well-aged wine and choice meat. There he will remove the cloud of gloom, the shadow of death that hangs over the earth. (Isaiah 25:6-7 NLT)

Jesus is going to remove the "cloud of gloom" and "shadow of death" that "hangs over the earth." I think that's such a perfect illustration of how the world is today. Here's a picture of what the restored current earth will be like during those 1,000 years that Jesus reigns.

> The wilderness and the dry land will be glad. The desert will rejoice and blossom like a rose. It will blossom abundantly, and rejoice even with joy and singing. ... Tell those who have a fearful heart, "Be strong! Don't be afraid! Behold, your God will come with vengeance, God's retribution. He will come and save you." ... Then the lame man will leap like a deer, and the tongue of the mute will sing; for waters will break out in the wilderness, and streams in the desert. The burning sand will become a pool, and the thirsty ground springs of water. Grass with reeds and rushes will be in the habitation of jackals, where they lay. (Isaiah 35:1-2, 4, 6-7)

You know, Satan likes to drop bombs of fear in his Battle of the Great Reset. You have no reason to fear all the scary things that Satan tells us about the earth's future. None of them are true. Is a ginormous asteroid going to come and split the earth in two? No. Jesus is going to reign on the existing planet for 1,000 years. Are there too many people on the planet for the planet to support everyone? No. God is infinite, which means he can create infinite resources for us.

God's Word is full of promises to provide for us (Matthew 6:25-33, Philippians 4:19). He did provide manna every day for 40 years for the Israelites (Exodus 16). Also remember that God desires everyone to be saved (1 Timothy 2:3-4). God always has room in his house (John

14:2). His house is truly all of the universe if you think about it.

Okay, now let's talk about the second component of the Great Reset that's an assault on the afterlife. The economic reset. This is an assault on God's economy in heaven. I know what you're thinking. Are you serious, there's an economy in heaven? Yes, there absolutely is. Let's discover how it works.

The Great Reset envisions a world in which no one owns anything. So, you don't own a house. Instead, you rent it. You also don't own anything in your house. You rent what you need when you need it. When you aren't using your house during the day, someone else can. You also don't own a car because you rely on public transportation. Are you picturing how Satan wants the world to work? Satan wants you to believe that you don't deserve to own or have anything. His tactic of stealing God's promises is at play here. The truth is that once you put your faith in Jesus for salvation, that you become an heir of God's estate.

> For as many as are led by the Spirit of God, these are children of God. For you didn't receive the spirit of bondage again to fear, but you received the Spirit of adoption, by whom we cry, "Abba! Father!" The Spirit himself testifies with our spirit that we are children of God; and if children, then heirs—heirs of God and joint heirs with Christ. (Romans 8:14-17)

In the Scripture above, the apostle Paul reveals that believers have been adopted by God. We're called "children of God" and "heirs of God." So, what exactly have we inherited? Well, eternal life is the main thing (Titus 3:7). The big ones that Satan is assaulting with the Great Reset are God's promises (Hebrews 6:12), a home (John 14:2-3), the kingdom of God (Matthew 25:34), and the entire world (Matthew 5:5).

> I saw a new heaven and a new earth.... I saw the holy city, New Jerusalem, coming down out of heaven from God.... I heard a loud voice out of heaven saying, "Behold, God's dwelling is with people; and he will dwell with them.... He will wipe away every tear from their eyes. Death will be no more; neither will there be mourning, nor crying, nor pain any more. ..."
> ... He said to me, "I am the Alpha and the Omega, the Beginning and the End. I will give freely to him who is thirsty from the spring of the water of life. He who overcomes, I will give him these things. I will be his God, and

he will be my son." (Revelation 21:1-4, 6-7)

As a believer, you're going to inherit property in the afterlife. All of it! And you're even going to have your own piece of heaven to call home (Isaiah 65:21, John 14:2-3). That's why Satan attacks property ownership. He doesn't want you to have any of it. He wants it all for himself.

Within Satan's assault on ownership, he's also attacking your uniqueness in the afterlife. He doesn't want you to think you're special. He doesn't want you to know that God has specific blessings just for you. So, Satan pushes the world to treat everyone exactly the same. No one can own anything because that would make some more blessed than others. No one should make more money than another because that's just not fair, is it? In fact, no one should even have to work. The government should support everyone with an equal living wage. All of these lies are assaults on your afterlife.

In God's kingdom, people are not equal. Some people are going to have more rewards than others. Jesus taught using parables. They are stories we can understand that illustrate truth. This particular parable that Jesus told is about God's kingdom. "When he had come" is referring to the king, who is Jesus.

> "When he had come back again, having received the kingdom, he commanded these servants, to whom he had given the money, to be called to him, that he might know what they had gained by conducting business. The first came before him, saying, 'Lord, your mina has made ten more minas.' He said to him, 'Well done, you good servant! Because you were found faithful with very little, you shall have authority over ten cities.' The second came, saying, 'Your mina, Lord, has made five minas.' So he said to him, 'And you are to be over five cities.' Another came, saying, 'Lord, behold, your mina, which I kept laid away in a handkerchief, for I feared you, because you are an exacting man. You take up that which you didn't lay down, and reap that which you didn't sow.' He said to him, 'Out of your own mouth I will judge you, you wicked servant!' ... He said to those who stood by, 'Take the mina away from him and give it to him who has the ten minas.' They said to him, 'Lord, he has ten minas!' 'For I tell you that to everyone who has, will more be given; but from him who doesn't have, even that which he has will be taken away from him.' " (Luke 19:15-22, 24-26)

So, we learn that one of the servants was rewarded with 10 cities, another with 5 cities, and one didn't get any at all. And in fact, the servant with 10 cities actually ended up with 11. What's this all about? God has given each of us a certain amount of "minas" per se. It's an illustration of how believers are going to be rewarded in the afterlife. To better understand how heaven's economy works, let's look at how the apostle Paul describes what God has given to each of us.

> God has apportioned to each person a measure of faith. For even as we have many members in one body, and all the members don't have the same function, so we, who are many, are one body in Christ, and individually members of one another, having gifts differing according to the grace that was given to us ... according to the proportion of our faith. (Romans 12:3-6)

We've each been given a "measure of faith." That's essentially your mina. What you do with your faith is where the reward comes in. The bigger your faith and the more bold things you do to bring glory to God, the bigger your reward is going to be in heaven. Now, before you complain about being given a small measure of faith and start making excuses about why you're not going to get a good reward, you should know that faith isn't static. You have to make it grow. You start with zero faith. The first step in earning some is to accept Jesus as your savior. Then you can earn more when your faith is tested (James 1:3-4), when you learn more about God and increase your trust in him (2 Peter 1:1-8), and by doing good deeds (James 2:14-26). And if you've given up something big for Jesus, the reward is 100 times as much (Matthew 19:29). For examples of faith, read Hebrews 11. It's the faith hall of fame.

I hope you also noticed in Jesus's parable that the servants who were rewarded also received authority over cities. Jesus did say that believers are going to reign with him (Revelation 20:6). The Bible mentions five crowns including the incorruptible crown for self-control (1 Corinthians 9:25), the crown of life for believers martyred for their faith (Revelation 2:10), the crown of glory for good leaders (1 Peter 5:2-4), the crown of righteousness for people looking forward to seeing Jesus (2 Timothy 4:8), and the crown of rejoicing for soul winners (1 Thessalonians 2:19-20). There very well could be other crowns, but those are the ones we know about. Be aware that Satan wants to steal your crown if you've already earned one (Revelation 3:11). God rewards us with responsibility, not with sitting around doing nothing all day. Satan's assault on this aspect of the afterlife is his lie that you don't have to work. Now, not everyone is going to get a crown in heaven. Some people are going to enter heaven and have nothing to show for it (1 Corinthians 3:11-15).

To defeat this lie, you must remember that whatever you choose to do in life, that you're ultimately working for Jesus and not for mankind (Colossians 3:23-24). But keep in mind that you cannot earn your way into heaven. Salvation is a gift from God that you just need to accept (Ephesians 2:8-9). And your success in this life, as measured by your wealth, career choice, or possessions, does not have any bearing on your afterlife. Your afterlife rewards all revolve around faith.

Don't fall for Satan's Great Reset delusion. Instead, look forward to Jesus's soon return when he'll restore creation to its perfect state. It really will be heaven on earth when that happens. If you've put your faith in Jesus, you'll be there with him, wearing white and hopefully with a crown, inheriting all of his promises.

Heaven isn't the only part of the afterlife that Satan is assaulting. He's also attacking the ones who currently live there, the deceased believers and holy angels. Join me in Part 3 of this book, and we'll explore this battle together.

PART 3

SATAN'S ASSAULT ON THOSE WHO LIVE IN HEAVEN

CHAPTER 8 - DEMONIC COMMUNICATION

The Antichrist will blaspheme God, God's dwelling which is heaven, and those who dwell there (Revelation 13:6). The ones who live there are believers who have died and holy angels. You're probably wondering what Satan's assault on those who are already in heaven has to do with you. In this chapter, we're going to discuss mankind's desire to commune with the dead. I think it's a natural thing to want to do. We all want to know what happens after death. We also want to know if the people we love are okay in the afterlife. The unknown is often scary. It seems like the best thing would be to ask someone who's already dead all about it. We think that would put our mind at ease. I'm sure it's something you've even contemplated yourself. Satan knows we want to do this, so he takes advantage of it.

So, what do people do when they want to talk to someone who's deceased? A few things come to mind. They hire a psychic or medium, they use a tool like a Ouija board or tarot cards, or they attempt to travel to the afterlife themselves using astral projection. Let's consider each one of these and what God's Word has to say about them.

We're going to start with psychics and mediums. If you aren't familiar with them, they are people who claim they can do things like communicate with the spirit world, talk to the deceased, channel the dead, make a ghost of the dead appear, and foretell your future. I used the word *claim* on purpose. That's because they aren't talking to your loved one. They're being deceived and so are you if you've sought their help for such things.

In these Scriptures below, we see that God commanded us not to consult with mediums or a whole host of people like them.

> " 'You shall not use enchantments, nor practice sorcery. ... Don't turn to those who are mediums, nor to the wizards. Don't seek them out, to be defiled by them. I am Yahweh your God.' " (Leviticus 19:26, 31)

> There shall not be found with you anyone who makes his son or his daughter to pass through the fire, one who uses divination, one who tells fortunes, or an enchanter, or a sorcerer, or a charmer, or someone who consults with a familiar spirit, or a wizard, or a necromancer. For whoever

does these things is an abomination to Yahweh. Because of these abominations, Yahweh your God drives them out from before you. ... For these nations that you shall dispossess listen to those who practice sorcery and to diviners; but as for you, Yahweh your God has not allowed you so to do. (Deuteronomy 18:10-12, 14)

So why would God forbid us from doing this? Wouldn't it be a good thing to get comfort by talking to a loved one who's already in heaven? After all, King Saul went to a medium so he could talk to the dead prophet Samuel and get advice (1 Samuel 28:3-25). Well, God further revealed to the Israelites when he was giving them these commands that a person consulting a medium was prostituting themselves (Leviticus 20:6). They were being unfaithful to God. In the verse below, the prophet Isaiah helps us understand what God expects us to do instead.

> When they tell you, "Consult with those who have familiar spirits and with the wizards, who chirp and who mutter," shouldn't a people consult with their God? Should they consult the dead on behalf of the living? (Isaiah 8:19)

When we seek advice, help, or comfort from a medium or someone deceased rather than God, we're committing adultery and acting like a prostitute. I know that seems harsh, but we're essentially saying we don't trust God to provide what we need. Whether that's answers or comfort or anything else we expect the medium or deceased person to provide. We're betraying God. We've put another before God. That's idolatry. God's first command in the Ten Commandments warned us against this (Deuteronomy 5:7). King Saul ended up dying because he consulted a medium; he was unfaithful toward God (1 Chronicles 10:13-14).

Now, I don't know if God will cause you to die if you consult a medium. But he's certainly protecting you from death by forbidding this type of communication. When we aren't worshiping God, the Bible tells us who we're really worshiping instead.

> Therefore, my beloved, flee from idolatry. ... But I say that the things which the Gentiles sacrifice, they sacrifice to demons and not to God, and I don't

desire that you would have fellowship with demons. You can't both drink the cup of the Lord and the cup of demons. You can't both partake of the table of the Lord and of the table of demons. (1 Corinthians 10:14, 20-21)

That's right, it's demons. God is protecting us from talking to demons and other evil spirits by telling us not to consult mediums. I know it's difficult to envision that consulting a psychic is really a type of sacrifice. Here's why it is. It goes back to what's due to God. God wants us to cast all of our burdens, worries, sorrow, you name it, onto him (Philippians 4:6-7, 1 Peter 5:7). That's our sacrifice to God. We're placing all of those things at his feet. We're supposed to depend on him. In return, he promises to comfort us and give us his peace that surpasses all understanding. So, do you see how taking an anxiety or need to someone deceased in exchange for comfort in return is actually offering up a sacrifice to a demon?

Satan is assaulting our afterlife when he pretends to be a deceased loved one. Why do people who consult psychics automatically assume they're hearing from the deceased or one of God's holy angels? Satan and his fallen angels are masquerading as the spirits of the deceased. This shouldn't surprise us. God told us that Satan likes to pretend to be an angel of the light (2 Corinthians 11:14-15). Which is exactly why this wouldn't be a holy angel pretending; they don't do that, they're holy and do not sin.

Perhaps you're still skeptical that psychics are conversing with demons because of your personal experience. Maybe you hired one and they told you things about the deceased that they couldn't have known, things that only the deceased would have known. Or maybe you saw a psychic on TV displaying this. Well, you need to realize that demons know a lot about us. It's their job to walk around the earth and watch us. They've been doing that for thousands of years. They are experts at it now. God told us that Satan himself prowls around like a lion (1 Peter 5:8). In the book of Job, we learn that Satan had been patrolling the earth and had been watching Job. So, we shouldn't be surprised that demons are able to pretend to be people.

However, please realize that Satan and demons cannot hear your thoughts and prayers. They are not all-knowing. That's reserved for God alone (Psalm 139:2). Only Jesus knows your innermost thoughts (Matthew 9:4). If you've consulted a psychic or thought about it because you want to talk to a deceased loved one, pray to God instead. If you know a loved one who's caught up in being a medium, pray to God for them. I know that prayer often doesn't feel like we're doing enough. Remember that God loves you. He will comfort you. God also loves the person you're praying for more than you do. He hasn't given up trying to reach them.

Now, we also need to consider the opposite of God's command. He forbids us from talking to the dead. The opposite is the dead talking to us. If a dead person talks to us, that means we're talking to it too, which we're not supposed to do, and which would encourage us to pursue it further. So, both talking to and being talked to by someone deceased are forbidden by God. There's a clear example of this that Jesus taught in the parable of the rich man and the beggar, Lazarus.

> "The beggar died, and he was carried away by the angels to Abraham's bosom. The rich man also died and was buried. In Hades, he lifted up his eyes, being in torment, and saw Abraham far off, and Lazarus at his bosom. ... He said, 'I ask you therefore, father, that you would send him to my father's house— for I have five brothers—that he may testify to them, so they won't also come into this place of torment.' But Abraham said to him, 'They have Moses and the prophets. Let them listen to them.' He said, 'No, father Abraham, but if one goes to them from the dead, they will repent.' He said to him, 'If they don't listen to Moses and the prophets, neither will they be persuaded if one rises from the dead.' "
> (Luke 16:22-23, 27-31)

The rich man died and went to the present hell. He could see Abraham in Abraham's Bosom and he asked Abraham to send Lazarus to his family so that Lazarus could warn them about the "place of torment." We learn that God sent the prophets for this purpose. We have all of God's Word. That should be enough to convince us of the truth and to warn us of judgment for not believing. If you can't believe the prophets, you're not going to believe if someone you know rose from the dead. Consider Jesus and how many don't believe he was resurrected.

So, if you think you've heard from a deceased loved one by any sort of means, I don't think you did. The deceased are forbidden from talking to us. It would have to be a really extraordinary circumstance for God to allow it. We're going to talk about that in a second. There are two possibilities regarding who really communicated with you. If you used a medium or the like, then we've established that you heard from a demon. If you prayed to God and then received some sort of special message bringing you comfort about your deceased loved one, then you heard from God. In either instance there's a way you can tell. The Bible tells us to test the spirits.

> Beloved, don't believe every spirit, but test the spirits, whether they are of God, because many false prophets have gone out into the world. By this you know the Spirit of God: every spirit who confesses that Jesus Christ has come in the flesh is of God, and every spirit who doesn't confess that Jesus Christ has come in the flesh is not of God; and this is the spirit of the Antichrist. (1 John 4:1-3)

If you're ever in the position in which you need to test a spirit, just ask them who Jesus is. A demon is going to lie to you. A spirit from God will tell you the truth, that Jesus is God in the flesh.

You know, the thought occurred to me that some of you reading this might have dabbled at being a medium. Or maybe you're thinking about doing it. Perhaps you used a Ouija board or tarot cards by yourself or with some friends. Just for fun you say. It doesn't matter what means you use to communicate with the dead, it's still forbidden. Using a tool would be considered witchcraft, sorcery, or a magic art. All of which are listed as forbidden. You are not going to find the answers you want this way. Only God knows your future (Isaiah 46:9-10). If you're a believer, God has a good plan for you that you can be hopeful about (Romans 8:28, Jeremiah 29:11). And it's God who's in control of the afterlife, who's able to comfort you about deceased loved ones, and who reveals what the afterlife is like.

There's a reason God doesn't want us dabbling in this space just for fun. It's because it makes us vulnerable to demonic possession. You must remember that in this war Satan is really after your soul. He wants to prevent you from getting to heaven by any means he can. Let's look at an encounter the apostle Paul had with a fortune teller.

> As we were going to prayer, a certain girl having a spirit of divination met us, who brought her masters much gain by fortune telling. Following Paul

and us, she cried out, "These men are servants of the Most High God, who proclaim to us a way of salvation!" She was doing this for many days. But Paul, becoming greatly annoyed, turned and said to the spirit, "I command you in the name of Jesus Christ to come out of her!" It came out that very hour. (Acts 16:16-18)

The girl was a fortune teller who was controlled by a demon, a "spirit of divination." Perhaps you think it would be cool to be possessed. I read that's actually a trend on social media these days. Well, you should be forewarned that demons oppress people. The girl above had masters; she was a slave. Jesus healed many demon-possessed people during his first coming. The demons tortured their victims. Some were blind, mute, cut themselves, and threw themselves into fire (Matthew 12:22, Mark 5:1-20, Matthew 17:14-20). Satan doesn't mess around. If you give him an inch, he's going to barge right in and take everything. This is why it's so important to stay away from any type of communication with the deceased. You must guard your soul. The way you do that is by putting your faith in Jesus. Then you'll receive his Holy Spirit as a seal and guarantee in return (Ephesians 1:13). God is greater than Satan and his evil demons (1 John 4:4). He's able to protect and keep you. You must also repent of what you've done and purge all the demonic communication items you have - Ouija board, tarot cards, crystal ball, or magic books (Acts 19:13-20).

Instead of playing around with talking to the dead, perhaps you've tried to actually go visit the dead via an out of body experience, astral projection, or soul travel. This is just as dangerous. Here's what a fellow Christian author, Ken Johnson, has to say about this. "Astral projection is the belief that a person can learn to fall into a type of meditative sleep that allows his or her soul to leave their body and travel in a spiritual plane of existence. The ancient church taught this phenomenon was simply a vision given to the person by a demon tricking them into believing they had actually left their body. The practitioner will eventually be led by the demonic visions to conclude that Christianity is false. The ancient church taught when the soul actually leaves the body, the body dies."[1]

This is not a new phenomenon. The ancient early church dealt with this too. You aren't really leaving your body, it's an illusion by the master of deception, Satan. If your spirit actually leaves your body, then you die (2 Corinthians 5:6-8). If you do this, a demon is your tour guide.

Now, I know that two people in the Bible had an experience like soul travel. Jesus's disciple John was taken up into heaven and saw what he wrote down in the book of Revelation (Revelation 4:1-2). And the apostle Paul was taken up into heaven and saw things so wonderful he wasn't allowed to tell us (2 Corinthians 12:1-6). In both instances, God took them to reveal something to them. Neither one of them initiated the travel. So, you shouldn't either. If God wants to show you something, he will.

Another phenomenon I want to address is people who see apparitions, ghosts, or spirits. There are numerous accounts of this. Don't scoff at it, or at least not all of it. Some of it is faked, especially questionable TV shows. But seeing spirits can be legit. It happened in the Bible. So, it can certainly happen today. People have even told me personal accounts of this happening to them. I believe them.

In the Bible we know that Jesus's disciples Peter, James, and John all saw the spirits of Moses and Elijah when Jesus was being transfigured (Matthew 17:1-3). We also know that dead righteous people were raised at Jesus's crucifixion and appeared to people in Jerusalem (Matthew 27:50-53). And King Saul really did get to speak with the spirit of the deceased Samuel when he consulted the medium (1 Samuel 28:3-25). Even though God forbid what Saul did, God let Samuel talk to Saul to rebuke him and tell him he was going to die. These were all instances of someone seeing a righteous deceased person. Someone who would be dwelling in heaven today. Now, these were also all very special circumstances. Based on God's Word, I don't believe anyone today is going to see the spirit of someone who is in the present heaven or present hell. That's because God wouldn't want to encourage us to seek out and communicate with the deceased or angels. He's not going to do anything that contradicts commands he's given us in the Bible. God also doesn't change his mind or beliefs (Numbers 23:19, Psalm 33:11). What he's communicated in the Bible about this is still his authoritative Word on it.

In today's day and age, I believe people either see the spirits of holy angels, spirits of fallen angels, or demons, or evil spirits. It's imperative that you be able to tell the difference.

Let's start with the holy angels. In the Bible, there are many instances of God's holy angels appearing to people. After Jesus's crucifixion angels appeared at his tomb. They shone like lightning and wore white robes (Matthew 28:2-5). When Jesus's disciple John saw an angel, he was so awestruck that he was compelled to bow down and worship it (Revelation 19:9-10). The angel told him not to. When an angel appeared to a bunch of shepherds at the birth of Jesus, they were all terrified (Luke 2:8-15). The angel told them not to fear because he was bringing good news. When the angel Gabriel appeared to Zechariah to tell him about his soon to be born son, John the Baptist, Zechariah although terrified didn't believe Gabriel (Luke 1:13-19). So, Gabriel told him he was sent by God. In fact, when Gabriel appeared to another prophet, Daniel, he told him he was sent by God as an answer to Daniel's prayer. Daniel was also terrified and fell down in fear (Daniel 8-9).

To sum it up, we know that seeing a holy angel will invoke awestruck fear and a desire to worship it. We also know that the angel will seek to comfort us and reassure us that they were sent by God. They won't pretend to be someone they aren't. They're doing their job. After all, they are ministering spirits for believers (Hebrews 1:14).

The *Ancient Book of Enoch* and the *Ancient Book of Jubilees*, historical books that we can learn a great deal from, tell us that evil spirits come from the dead Nephilim. Their spirits roam the earth. They were the giants. The human-angel hybrids.[2] The Bible also refers to them as devils or demons. However, some Bible translations use the words *demon* and *fallen angel* interchangeably. Regardless of if it's a spirit or an angel, they are all fallen and evil. Fallen angels, demons, and evil spirits are easy. They're going to act like Satan.

You learned all about Satan's behavior and tactics in Part 1. They're going to blaspheme God (Revelation 13:6). That's what they do, tell lies. I also don't believe that demons or evil spirits are going to shine like the holy angels. The holy angels are in God's presence. It's God's glory that they're reflecting. Even Moses's face shone after he was in God's presence (Exodus 34:29-30). The demons and evils spirits aren't in God's presence, so they aren't going to be radiant. You won't be awe inspired to worship them. I have no doubt you'll still be terrified by seeing one though. They'll also likely appear as someone they aren't. That's what Satan likes to do, pretend to be an angel of the light (2 Corinthians 11:14). He's a master illusionist. It's not a stretch for him or the other fallen angels to pretend to be anything, is it?

There are several ways you can rid yourself of an evil spirit or demon. Invoke Jesus's name against it (Luke 10:17). Even people who didn't follow Jesus were able to cast out demons in his name (Mark 9:38-39). Pray to Jesus and ask him to remove it (Mark 9:29). Sometimes you may need to pray, fast, and have awesome faith in order to cast it out (Matthew 17:19-21). Find a believer who is strong in the faith, perhaps an elder at your church, and have them pray for you.

I hope you have a better understanding of how Satan is assaulting the afterlife by assaulting the deceased. In the next chapter, we're going to continue exploring his assault on the deceased by focusing on unanswered prayers.

CHAPTER 9 – UNANSWERED PRAYERS

When you pray, who do you pray to? Is it God or Jesus? Perhaps it's Jesus's mother Mary, the angel Michael, your deceased father, or one of Jesus's disciples like Peter. Do you ever pray for the salvation of a loved one who's no longer living? You know, some of these prayers are not going to be answered. Satan is deceiving you and assaulting those who live in heaven by convincing you to send prayers to and for afterlife dwellers instead of to God for the living. Satan's assaulting the afterlife by robbing God of prayers.

Let's start our conversation with who we should be praying to. Jesus taught his disciples how to pray. This is what he said to do.

> "But you, when you pray, enter into your inner room, and having shut your door, pray to your Father who is in secret; and your Father who sees in secret will reward you openly. ... Pray like this: 'Our Father in heaven, may your name be kept holy.' " (Matthew 6:6, 9)

We're to pray to our "Father in heaven." That's God. If you pray to anyone other than God, you're damaging your relationship with God. As discussed in the prior chapter, it's committing idolatry. Make all of your petitions to God (Philippians 4:6).

This isn't a new assault by Satan. He's been deceiving people with this lie about praying to deceased ancestors for thousands of years. The prophet Isaiah wrote about praying to or consulting the dead. God explained that people should pray to and consult God.

> When they tell you, "Consult with those who have familiar spirits and with the wizards, who chirp and who mutter," shouldn't a people consult with their God? Should they consult the dead on behalf of the living? Turn to the law and to the covenant! (Isaiah 8:19-20)

This form of ancestor worship can often lead people to create physical idols. We read in the Old Testament that this was a common sin. The people created idols that were carved likenesses of ancestors, or they kept something belonging to an ancestor. Then they would bow down and worship and pray to those things (Isaiah 44:9-20).

Perhaps you've made an idol without realizing it. There's new technology that lets you upload a person's social media history and other things they've said or written. An artificial intelligence (AI) then takes that information and is able to mimic the person in conversation. So, you can have a chat with the AI who is posing as the person. I can see this gaining popularity through the fake resurrection of a deceased person or loved one. Don't be tempted into doing it. It's a modern-day idol.

Something else that seems popular these days is jewelry and other keepsakes that are made with the ashes of the deceased. Now, having that isn't the problem. If you're talking to the trinket as though your loved one can hear you, then you've created yourself a modern-day idol. The thing you're praying to can't hear you or help you (Habakkuk 2:18-20, Revelation 9:20).

I know this one is a challenging truth. Some of you might be consoled when you pray to King David while reading one of his psalms. Many of you likely get comfort by talking to your deceased loved one while looking at a photo of them. As much as this may hurt, you need to know that the deceased can't hear you. In the prior chapter, we discussed that God forbids communication with the dead. That communication goes both ways.

Remember the parable of the rich man and Lazarus (Luke 16:19-31)? The rich man went to the present hell and desperately wanted to send a message to his living family. He knew he wasn't able to. So, he asked Abraham, who was in Abraham's Bosom, to send Lazarus. Abraham told the rich man that his family had all of God's truth that the prophets wrote down. No message was getting sent from the afterlife back to the living.

Instead of trying to receive comfort from something that can't provide it, let God comfort you (Matthew 5:4, 2 Corinthians 1:3). It's one of his specialties. If you have a message for your deceased loved one, tell it to God. God will hear you and will pass it along if that's his will.

Now, what about praying to an angel? Is it okay to pray to them since they work for God, probably aren't as busy as God, and they're messengers after all? Well, we've already established that praying to anyone or anything other than God is not okay. Just to clarify, here's a Scripture that specifically refers to angels. Jesus's disciple John is the one the angel is speaking to.

> And the angel said to me, "Write this: Blessed are those who are invited to the wedding feast of the Lamb." And he added, "These are true words that come from God." Then I fell down at his feet to worship him, but he said, "No, don't worship me. I am a servant of God, just like you and your brothers and sisters who testify about their faith in Jesus. Worship only God." (Revelation 19:9-10 NLT)

You know, Satan is assaulting the holy angels in heaven when he tells lies about them. His lie that angels are at your service is not true. So don't pray to them because prayer is a form of worship. As we learn in the verses above, the angels are in God's service, not ours. The angel rightly told John to "worship only God." A good example of how the angels operate where prayer is concerned is Daniel's encounter with the angel Gabriel. Daniel was fervently praying to God seeking understanding about a prophecy Jeremiah wrote. That's when the angel Gabriel showed up and told Daniel that God heard his prayer and had commanded Gabriel to deliver a reply to him (Daniel 9:2-22).

So far, we've covered that God only answers prayers directed toward him. If you're praying to anyone or anything else, your prayer is going unanswered. There's another type of unanswered prayer we need to address. It's praying for a deceased person's salvation. I know, this is going to be another hard truth to swallow. Perhaps someone you care about died with their salvation in question. You're not sure they were a believer and are in heaven. So, you pray to God that he saves that person. Or maybe you believe your deceased loved one is stuck in a temporary purgatory type place and that you need to pray for them so they can move on to heaven.

You know, praying for deceased people can easily lead to wanting to do something for them or offer something to them. Prayer leads to other acts of worship, like sacrifice. Before you freak out and say you haven't killed anything for your deceased loved one, know that sacrifice involves many things. Consider your time, your money, and other material things. We sacrifice to God regularly when we commit time to pray to him, read our Bible, and go to church. I believe this is what Satan's assault on this aspect of the afterlife is really about. Satan wants you spending your time and money on things you shouldn't be doing, that God forbids, and that make you ineffective as a believer.

Satan is heavily promoting this lie about praying both to and for the dead. There's a popular festival in many parts of the world, it goes by Dia De Los Muertos here in New Mexico.[1] It means day of the dead. It's celebrated right after Halloween. People who celebrate it believe they can communicate with the dead once a year. They build altars for deceased where they place pictures of them and leave offerings which entice them to come and that'll sustain them in the afterlife, like food or toys. They believe the deceased hear their prayers to them and for them on this special day. A recent animated movie depicted this festival, *Coco*.[2] Do you see what Satan's done? He's assaulted the afterlife by getting people to pray, worship, and offer sacrifices to and for the deceased.

Let's look at some biblical truths to help us understand why these prayers for the deceased are going unanswered.

> If anyone sees his brother sinning a sin not leading to death, he shall ask, and God will give him life for those who sin not leading to death. There is sin leading to death. I don't say that he should make a request concerning this. (1 John 5:16)

In the Scripture above, John tells us that we shouldn't pray for someone committing the sin that leads to death. So, what's that sin?

> Everyone who speaks a word against the Son of Man will be forgiven, but those who blaspheme against the Holy Spirit will not be forgiven. (Luke 12:10)

Every single sin you can think of can be forgiven by Jesus, except one. It's "blaspheme against the Holy Spirit." Gosh, what does that mean? Well, it's when you refuse to accept Jesus's sacrifice for your salvation. Jesus is the only way into heaven. If you refuse to put your faith in him, then you don't get his Holy Spirit. Instead, you've disregarded the Holy Spirit, you've considered it worthless, you've blasphemed it. So, we're told not to pray for people who are adamant unbelievers and have hardened their hearts against Jesus. This is important because it applies to the living and the dead. Here's why.

> Inasmuch as it is appointed for men to die once, and after this, judgment. (Hebrews 9:27)

When you die, you don't go to a temporary holding place to await judgment or to have your sins cleansed. The concept of purgatory is entirely unbiblical. It's a deception from Satan. Here's how the Catholic encyclopedia defines purgatory: "Purgatory in accordance with Catholic teaching is a place or condition of temporal punishment for those who, departing this life in God's grace, are not entirely free from venial faults, or have not fully paid the satisfaction due to their transgressions. ... That temporal punishment is due to sin, even after the sin itself has been pardoned by God."3

When you die, you go to the present hell or the present heaven. You can't change your eternal destination once you die. Consider the rich man and Lazarus again. Keep in mind that Jesus himself told this account. If the rich man could have changed his fate, don't you think that would have been his request to Abraham? He would have asked Abraham to send Lazarus to tell his family to pray for him so that he could be transferred from torment to heaven. Yet that's not what he asked. The rich man knew his fate was sealed. The apostle Paul confirmed this when he told believers that to be absent from the body is to be present with God (2 Corinthians 5:8). Furthermore, there is only one advocate that each of us has in the afterlife. That's Jesus Christ (1 John 2:1, 1 Timothy 2:5). Jesus loves your deceased loved one more than you do. Remember that he willingly died to save everyone. If you think you can advocate for someone who's deceased, then you're considering yourself equal to God in the flesh. Yikes! There's no wonder the prayer is going unanswered.

Let's consider another Scripture from Revelation that might be causing some confusion.

> I saw a great white throne and him who sat on it, from whose face the earth and the heaven fled away. There was found no place for them. I saw the dead, the great and the small, standing before the throne, and they opened books. Another book was opened, which is the book of life. The dead were judged out of the things which were written in the books, according to their works. ... If anyone was not found written in the book of life, he was cast into the lake of fire. (Revelation 20:11-12, 15)

At the great white throne judgment, the only people being judged are those who didn't place their faith in Jesus. They are the people who are in the present hell, the place below the earth that we discussed in a prior chapter. These people don't have Jesus's Holy Spirit. Their names aren't in his Book of Life. So, they're judged "according to their works." They aren't judged according to your works, or by your prayers for them after they died. They are judged by their own works. Now, the only work that counts is Jesus's work on the cross because that's the only thing that takes away our sin (Colossians 2:13-14). All it takes is one sin to keep you out of heaven. And if you think you've lived a perfect life without sin, think again. We're all sinners by default because we inherited Adam's original sin (Romans 5:12). And Jesus confirmed that no one is good, we're all sinners (Mark 10:18, Romans 3:23). So, none of these deceased people will have a work that will get them into heaven. So, they're sent to the eternal hell. And therein lies where I think the confusion comes from. Some people think a deceased person can move from the present hell to the eternal heaven through the prayers and offerings of the living. No, that's not the case. Everyone in the present hell is going to the eternal hell.

I know that's really hard for some of you to hear. I know you're concerned about a loved one who died that you might not see again. Take comfort in God. Don't lose hope for your loved one, they may have said a quick silent prayer for salvation right before they passed. Or maybe they accepted Jesus as their savior when they were a teenager and just didn't walk with God after that. People like that will still be saved, they just might not have any treasure or glory to give to God when they get to the present heaven (1 Corinthians 3:13-15). We're going to be surprised by who we see in heaven. When we get to heaven, if we don't see our loved ones there, I'm confident that we aren't going to be sad. God tells us that there's no pain or sorrow or tears in heaven (Isaiah 25:8, Revelation 7:17, 21:4). So that means we'll be at peace with the decision our loved one made. I know it's hard to comprehend, but that's how God's peace works. It's beyond our comprehension (Philippians 4:7).

Real quick, there's another aspect of the purgatory deception that I need to address. It's about dying as a believer and going to purgatory because of sins that you haven't paid for. It's a big fat lie from Satan! Jesus paid your sin debt in full. On the cross he said his work was finished (John 19:30). Once you ask Jesus for forgiveness of your sins, and put your faith in him, that's it, there's nothing else you need to do to be saved. There is no longer any condemnation against you (Romans 8:1).

Instead of praying for the dead or to the dead, God wants us to pray for the living (1 Timothy 2:1-4). He wants everyone to be saved. That's why he tells us to intercede for the living. These are the prayers that really matter. These are the prayers that Satan's assault is trying to keep us from because God will answer them.

Continue with me in the upcoming Part 4 of this book as we examine a number of ways in which Satan is assaulting future citizens of heaven. That's you, you know!

PART 4

SATAN'S ASSAULT ON FUTURE CITIZENS OF HEAVEN

CHAPTER 10 - I AM CHRIST

If you've put your faith in Jesus for salvation, then you are considered a citizen of heaven (Philippians 3:20). Satan doesn't want anyone to become a citizen of heaven. So, he wages war against all people to deceive us about what citizens of heaven are like, do, feel, you name it. He doesn't want you to know the truth about who you'll really be in the afterlife and how to get to heaven in the first place. These are the assaults we're going to be discussing in this Part 4 of the book.

Satan has a particular fury toward believers because we're already citizens of heaven. I think that's why one of his primary assaults on the afterlife attacks our faith in Jesus and the only way to heaven (John 14:6). You may have heard it called Christ consciousness, cosmic consciousness, or even being one with Christ. Satan's lie is that anyone can attain heaven and salvation by tapping into their higher consciousness because each of us is already divine. We just don't realize it.

Here are some things Rhonda Byrne, author of the popular book *The Secret* teaches: "You are god in a physical body... You are all power... You are the creator... No matter who you thought you were, now you know the Truth of Who You Really Are. You are the master of the universe. You are the heir to the kingdom. You are the perfection of life. And now you know The Secret."[1]

You know, she's not the only one teaching this. If you've ever watched an episode of *The Oprah Winfrey Show* then you know exactly what I'm talking about. Here's something Oprah said during an interview with Eckhart Tolle, a popular new age spirituality author, as they discussed his book, *A New Earth*: "Jesus," said Oprah, "came to show us Christ-consciousness."[2] And here's something Eckhart teaches: "The true meaning of Christmas is that the very Being that you are is Truth. This is what Jesus meant when he said, 'I am the way and the truth and the life.' Jesus speaks of the inner essence identity of every human being. Some Christian writers call this the 'Christ within.' The real meaning of Christmas is to find that essential self that is universally experienced as the Christ within no matter what your cultural or religious upbringing is."[3]

I hope you're starting to see that this is the same lie that Satan told

Eve. Her belief in this got her kicked out of the garden. He told her that she could be like God. Satan is peddling that same deception here. That you can be like God if you just tap into your Christ consciousness and realize that you're already him. Seriously? I really struggle to see how so many people are buying into this. I mean, do you think that you're Jesus? I've put my faith in Jesus for salvation. That doesn't make me equal to Jesus. As a believer, God has placed the Holy Spirit inside of me as a seal, like my passport into heaven (Ephesians 1:13). That doesn't make me the actual Holy Spirit. There's a big difference between the two. Possessing something isn't the same thing as being that something. Satan doesn't want you to know the way to heaven. He wants you looking in the wrong place.

You know, Jesus warned us about this false teaching.

> As he sat on the Mount of Olives, the disciples came to him privately, saying, "Tell us, when will these things be? What is the sign of your coming, and of the end of the age?" Jesus answered them, "Be careful that no one leads you astray. For many will come in my name, saying, 'I am the Christ,' and will lead many astray. ... Then if any man tells you, 'Behold, here is the Christ!' or, 'There!' don't believe it. For false christs and false prophets will arise, and they will show great signs and wonders, so as to lead astray, if possible, even the chosen ones. Behold, I have told you beforehand. If therefore they tell you, 'Behold, he is in the wilderness,' don't go out; or 'Behold, he is in the inner rooms,' don't believe it." (Matthew 24:3-5, 23-26)

This entire conversation with Jesus started because his disciples wanted to know more about Jesus's second coming, the "end of the age." The very first thing that Jesus told them to watch out for is people who say, "I am the Christ." It's a hallmark of the end times. This is exactly what's happening today. Here's something else really fascinating about this Scripture. Notice the last sentence where Jesus says don't look for him in "inner rooms." Well, according to Strong's definition it means a secret chamber. I don't think it could fit more perfectly as a warning against what books like *The Secret* are teaching. Jesus doesn't want you looking for him like some secret inside yourself, inside your own inner room. Jesus isn't a secret. He made the truth about himself as plain as day.

Jesus Christ is God in the flesh and the creator of all things, including you. You are not one with creation or one with Jesus. You are unique. And God is completely separate from his creation.

> Christ is the visible image of the invisible God. He existed before anything was created and is supreme over all creation, for through him God created everything in the heavenly realms and on earth. He made the things we can see and the things we can't see—such as thrones, kingdoms, rulers, and authorities in the unseen world. Everything was created through him and for him. ... Yet now he has reconciled you to himself through the death of Christ in his physical body. As a result, he has brought you into his own presence, and you are holy and blameless as you stand before him without a single fault. But you must continue to believe this truth and stand firmly in it. Don't drift away from the assurance you received when you heard the Good News. (Colossians 1:15-16, 22-23 NLT)

Like the apostle Paul revealed in this Scripture above, you must continue to believe the truth about Jesus. Jesus died for your sins and then rose from the dead, proving that he's God and has the power over life and death. Don't let some new teaching pull you away from the truth just because it sounds fancy or sounds really hard to achieve, and you think salvation and heaven must be spiritual and really hard to attain.

You know this brings me to another assault on the afterlife that's happening with this Christ consciousness business. It spiritualizes heaven and you. It's one of the lies I exposed in Chapter 5. Heaven isn't a state of mind. It's a real physical place. You are not a spiritual being who's just having a temporary bodily existence and who's going to be absorbed into some grand cosmic energy when you die. That's the nonsense that the *Star Wars* movies promote. You're not one with the force and you're not going to become part of the force at your death. You're not going to be a spirit floating around the universe. You're not going to transform into light or become a star. You're not going to join with the spirits of others and inhabit your living descendants, either. This whole spiritual way of looking at yourself is just a bunch of hot air from Satan. He's trying to deceive you about who you really are.

Remember that you are a child of God. When God created Adam, he created his body first and then breathed life into him (Genesis 2:7).

And just like Adam, you were created in God's very own image.

> For you are all children of God, through faith in Christ Jesus. (Galatians 3:26)

> God created man in his own image. In God's image he created him; male and female he created them. (Genesis 1:27)

This is why Satan spiritualizes you and your afterlife. He's jealous that you look like God because he doesn't. He doesn't want you to know that you were created special. And you're not going to suddenly stop looking like God's image when you get to heaven, either. You are going to have a real physical body in heaven. Even Job, you know, the one Satan directly assaulted and who lived thousands of years ago, knew that he would see God face-to-face in his own body (Job 19:26).

Now, I need to clarify something. If you're a believer, then you'll get your new glorified body at the rapture (more about the rapture in Chapter 19). If you die before the rapture, you'll still get your new body at the rapture. You'll have some sort of temporary body in the present heaven until the rapture happens.

In the parable Jesus told about the rich man and Lazarus, there are references to body parts, like Lazarus's finger and the rich man's tongue, and bodily desires, like the rich man's thirst (Luke 16:24). Also consider the believers that'll be martyred during the tribulation period. When they go to the present heaven, they're wearing clothes and waving palm branches (Revelation 7:9-14). All of these people in the present heaven have some type of body because they're able to wear clothes and interact with the physical environment. Spirits wouldn't be able to do that. All believers will have their glorified bodies for the millennial reign with Jesus on earth and for the eternal heaven, the new earth. Here are some things the Bible reveals about our new forever bodies.

> For our citizenship is in heaven, from where we also wait for a Savior, the Lord Jesus Christ, who will change the body of our humiliation to be conformed to the body of his glory. (Philippians 3:20-21)

First off, your body is going to be real. It'll be like the body of Jesus's glory. That refers to his resurrection body. And here we have a good description of Jesus after he rose from the grave.

> Jesus himself stood among them, and said to them, "Peace be to you." But they were terrified and filled with fear, and supposed that they had seen a spirit. He said to them, "Why are you troubled? Why do doubts arise in your hearts? See my hands and my feet, that it is truly me. Touch me and see, for a spirit doesn't have flesh and bones, as you see that I have." When he had said this, he showed them his hands and his feet. While they still didn't believe for joy, and wondered, he said to them, "Do you have anything here to eat?" They gave him a piece of a broiled fish and some honeycomb. He took them, and ate in front of them. (Luke 24:36-43)

Jesus appeared to his disciples. As you can see, they assumed he was a spirit, a ghost. But he told them to touch him and see for themselves that he was indeed real. And if that wasn't enough, he ate some fish with them. He had a glorified body of "flesh and bone." You will too. In heaven, you'll be able to eat and drink and touch and interact with the physical world just like you do now. And yes, you'll have clothes too (Revelation 19:8). If you're skeptical because Jesus appeared to his disciples on earth and you think this must not apply to heaven, well Jesus told them before he died that they would all be eating and drinking with him in his kingdom, at his father's table (Luke 22:29-30). He was talking about heaven. There's even going to be a wedding feast there (Revelation 19:9).

Your new body is called glorified because it's "imperishable" and immortal (1 Corinthians 15:42-53). It's going to last forever. In case you didn't notice in the Scripture above, you are also going to look like yourself and act like yourself. The disciples recognized that it was Jesus. You're also going to retain your birth gender. No one referred to the resurrected Jesus as a female or as an it. God created us all male and female. That doesn't change. Perhaps you also noticed that Jesus still had his scars. The Bible doesn't give us specifics about which traits of ours will transfer into heaven, but it looks like some of them will. Maybe you've got a unique birthmark. There's a good possibility you'll still have it in heaven. But be assured that there isn't going to be any disease or decay in heaven. So, any defects, injury, or illness you have that limits you or causes you pain won't be going with you to heaven

(Revelation 21:4). You're getting a new body.

I'm sure your mind is coming up with all sorts of questions about your new body. Are you wondering what age you'll look like? You know, the Bible doesn't say. It makes me wonder what age Adam and Eve looked like when God created them. Perhaps we'll look the same age they did. Then again, maybe some of us will look older than others. Either way, you're going to love how you look because you'll look better than you ever have. In fact, everything about your new body is going to be better. Consider all of your senses and how each of them will be more than what you experience today.

However, better doesn't mean perfect. You're not going to have the attributes that God has. God is all-knowing and all-powerful, for example. You aren't going to be either of those. Your new body won't be weak, but it won't be all-powerful either. You're also not going to be perfect at doing everything. If you think you're going to suddenly be the best at whatever skill or sport you're passionate about, I don't believe that's the case. Just think about how boring it would be if you suddenly knew how to do everything perfectly. You're going to live forever. You'll have eternity to learn and master anything you want. In fact, it'll be a lot easier than it is now because our minds and bodies will function superbly.

I hope that I've got you thinking about heaven now and the wonderful body and experiences that await you. That's exactly what Jesus wants you thinking about.

> If then you were raised together with Christ, seek the things that are above, where Christ is, seated on the right hand of God. Set your mind on the things that are above, not on the things that are on the earth. (Colossians 3:1-2)

That's also where you'll find him. In the heavens "above," not some secret place within yourself.

CHAPTER 11 - THE UNDEAD APOCALYPSE

What do you think one of the most watched cable TV shows is? In 2014, the season premiere for the fifth season of *The Walking Dead* had 17.3 million viewers. If you haven't heard of it, I'm sure you guessed that it's about the zombie apocalypse. It's so popular it has its own universe, like Marvel, and after the final season 11 airs in the fall of 2021, spin off shows are already in the works.[1]

Perhaps you've heard of this next franchise. Of the top 10 horror video games, 7 of them belong to the *Resident Evil* franchise. Those games catapulted the movies by the same name to the highest grossing horror movies of all time. And now it has a TV series in production.[2]

If zombies aren't your thing, how about vampires? Have you seen *Dracula, Buffy The Vampire Slayer, Interview With The Vampire, Supernatural,* or any of the *Twilight* movies?[3] From 1999 to 2019, vampire movies actually outperformed all other monster movies at the box office, including zombies, earning more than $2 billion.[4] The undead are certainly money makers in entertainment.

In case you've never seen a monster movie like those, let me explain what the undead are. Zombies are dead people who've been reanimated, typically because of a virus or genetic engineering. They're like walking corpses who continue to decay. They prey on the living by desiring to eat people. If bitten by a zombie, you become a zombie too. Vampires are similar in many ways. They're a dead person come back to life after being bitten by a vampire. They also prey on the living by desiring to drink their blood. Now, unlike zombies, vampires typically have beautiful bodies and are completely themselves. They're often depicted as living hundreds of years and being trapped on earth, their souls unable to move on. Both of these mythical undead creatures are being used by Satan to assault your afterlife.

I know what you're thinking. You think it's silly that I included a chapter on the undead apocalypse because everyone knows this stuff isn't real. Well, it's more real than you think when you factor in science. Here are some recent headlines.

"Scientists Are Giving Dead Brains New Life. What Could Go Wrong?"[5]

> "Resurrected: A Controversial Trial To Bring The Dead Back To Life"[6]
> "Pig Brains Partially Revived Hours After Death—What It Means For People"[7]
> "Can Blood From Young People Slow Aging? Silicon Valley Has Bet Billions It Will"[8]

People want to live forever. When people don't know that Jesus offers immortality, or if they don't want to attain immortality Jesus's way, then they'll try to achieve it any way they can. Zombies and vampires are the dead brought back to life. It's no wonder that scientists are conducting experiments that appear to be inspired by these undead. And just because these undead aren't real doesn't mean it's not having a huge impact on society. Just think about those movie stats I revealed earlier. Or how about Halloween and how many kids dress up as zombies and vampires pretending to be them for the day. Do you think that's okay? You might have a different opinion after understanding how Satan is using these undead monsters to assault your afterlife.

The first aspect of Satan's assault that I'd like to address is bringing the dead back to life and what they're like afterwards. There's a difference between reanimation and resurrection. To *reanimate* means to regain vitality, but there's a lack of consciousness. On the other hand, *resurrection* is bringing someone back to life, consciousness and all. Even if scientists figure out how to reanimate a body, I want to assure you that it won't have a consciousness. Contrary to what Satan wants you to think, you cannot become a zombie.

You are body, soul, and spirit (1 Thessalonians 5:23). As we've discussed, when you die, your soul, the part of you that's you, goes to your eternal destination. Either the present hell or the present heaven (Hebrews 9:27). So, that leaves your body and spirit. Here, we learn that without a spirit, the body is dead.

> The body apart from the spirit is dead. (James 2:26)

A person can have the Holy Spirit from God or the spirit of the world from Satan and his fallen angels (1 Corinthians 2:12). So once a body dies, one of those spirits is required to bring it back to life. But here's a key truth. Satan doesn't have power over death. Jesus does! He's "the Son" in this Scripture.

> Because God's children are human beings—made of flesh and blood—the Son also became flesh and blood. For only as a human being could he die, and only by dying could he break the power of the devil, who had the power of death. Only in this way could he set free all who have lived their lives as slaves to the fear of dying. (Hebrews 2:14-15 NLT)

There isn't any account in the Bible of Satan resurrecting someone. He's certainly going to fake a resurrection in the tribulation period with the Antichrist though because he wants people to think he's God (Revelation 13:3, 2 Thessalonians 2:9). Just contemplate this for a second. If Satan had the power over death, he'd be able to save himself, wouldn't he? After all that's what Jesus proved with his resurrection. If Satan had the power over death, Jesus never would have risen from the dead. If Satan had the power over death, none of us would be living because he hates our guts. He'd kill all of us and take over the planet. You alive is proof that Satan has no power over death. If Satan had the power of death, he wouldn't be assaulting the afterlife because he'd be the one in control of it. That's his ultimate desire, to replace God and take over heaven. So, there you have it, Satan's zombie apocalypse isn't going to happen.

If that's not enough to convince you, consider that Jesus resurrected, not reanimated, several people during his first coming. You see, Jesus literally said in a conversation with Martha, Lazarus's sister, that he's the resurrection.

> Jesus said to her, "I am the resurrection and the life. He who believes in me will still live, even if he dies. Whoever lives and believes in me will never die. Do you believe this?" (John 11:25-26)

Jesus has this power of resurrection because he has the power of life and the power over souls (Matthew 10:28). Other than his own resurrection (John 20), the most famous is when Jesus resurrected Lazarus from the grave when he'd been dead for four days already.

> Jesus therefore, again groaning in himself, came to the tomb. Now it was

a cave, and a stone lay against it. Jesus said, "Take away the stone." Martha, the sister of him who was dead, said to him, "Lord, by this time there is a stench, for he has been dead four days." Jesus said to her, "Didn't I tell you that if you believed, you would see God's glory?" So they took away the stone from the place where the dead man was lying. Jesus lifted up his eyes and said, "Father, I thank you that you listened to me. I know that you always listen to me, but because of the multitude standing around I said this, that they may believe that you sent me." When he had said this, he cried with a loud voice, "Lazarus, come out!" He who was dead came out, bound hand and foot with wrappings, and his face was wrapped around with a cloth. ... Then, six days before the Passover, Jesus came to Bethany, where Lazarus was, who had been dead, whom he raised from the dead. So they made him a supper there. Martha served, but Lazarus was one of those who sat at the table with him. (John 11:38-44, 12:1-2)

Jesus also raised a dead girl (Mark 5:21-43) and the son of a widow (Luke 7:11-17). Since Jesus has the power over death, he's able to give it to others if he wants. So, his disciples, Peter and Paul, were able to resurrect people too (Acts 9:36-43, Acts 20:7-12). All of those people who were resurrected resumed their life on earth. They weren't zombies who were bodies without a spirit or soul. That's because Jesus returned both the person's soul and God's Spirit to their body when he resurrected them. Obviously, Jesus also restored Lazarus's body. He didn't look like a zombie. He also didn't act like an unthinking zombie. As you can see above, Lazarus was himself. His sisters recognized him and were with him after his resurrection. He even ate supper with Jesus a few days later. He clearly had a consciousness.

Here's another good example of retained memories and consciousness after death. In the Scripture below, Jesus is the one who opened the fifth seal. This event takes place during the tribulation period.

> When he opened the fifth seal, I saw underneath the altar the souls of those who had been killed for the Word of God, and for the testimony of the Lamb which they had. They cried with a loud voice, saying, "How long, Master, the holy and true, until you judge and avenge our blood on those who dwell on the earth?" (Revelation 6:9-10)

These are the believers who will be martyred during the tribulation. They know they were murdered, and they remember. They also have some knowledge of what's happening on the earth since they ask, "how long?" We also know there's retained memory in our heavenly afterlife because we all have to give an account of the things we did on earth (Romans 14:12). And recall from the parable about the rich man and Lazarus (a different Lazarus than the resurrected one) that the rich man who went to the present hell had consciousness, remembered his life on earth, and remembered Lazarus (Luke 16:19-31).

As for what your body is going to look like in the afterlife, at the resurrection, we've already discussed that it's glorified. It'll be like Jesus's body after his resurrection. It'll be suitable for eternal life. If you've put your faith in Jesus, your resurrected body won't ever die or decay. The second death, the lake of fire, isn't for you (Revelation 20:6, 14). It'll be healed of whatever ailment it had on earth as well. You're going to look amazing! I hope you now realize that Satan's zombie propaganda about the undead being grotesque unthinkers isn't legit.

Let's move on to how Satan uses the undead to mock not only the salvation that Jesus offers everyone, but also wonderful promises that we have in heaven. Both vampires and zombies prey on the living. They eat them or drink their blood. This is a clear-cut assault against Jesus. See for yourself.

> Jesus therefore said to them, "Most certainly I tell you, unless you eat the flesh of the Son of Man and drink his blood, you don't have life in yourselves. He who eats my flesh and drinks my blood has eternal life, and I will raise him up at the last day." (John 6:53-54)

Jesus tells us to eat his flesh and drink his blood. In fact, he often referred to himself as food, like the Bread of Life (John 6:48) and living water (John 4:7-14). The apostle Paul helps us understand what Jesus means.

> The Lord Jesus on the night in which he was betrayed took bread. When he had given thanks, he broke it and said, "Take, eat. This is my body, which is broken for you. Do this in memory of me." In the same way he also took the cup after supper, saying, "This cup is the new covenant in my blood. Do this, as often as you drink, in memory of me." For as often

as you eat this bread and drink this cup, you proclaim the Lord's death until he comes. (1 Corinthians 11:23-26)

Jesus sacrificed his life so that we can live forever. If you believe what Jesus did with his body and his blood, then you are saved and can live in heaven. That's how he became our Bread of Life. When we participate in Communion, we're remembering that sacrifice and thanking Jesus for all that he's done. But it's even more than that. Jesus is the Word, the Bible (John 1:1-18). He wants you to know all about him and all the promises he has in store for you. Jesus wants you to fill yourself up with him. So, Satan is clearly assaulting the way to heaven with this business about the undead preying on people.

Satan is also attacking God's promises for you in the heavenly afterlife. You see, God promises that we'll have food to eat and plenty to drink in heaven. In fact, there's hidden manna which is the bread of the angels (Revelation 2:17, Psalm 78:24-25), the various fruits that come from the Tree of Life (Revelation 2:7), rivers of living water (Revelation 7:16-17), and even a wedding feast (Revelation 19:9).

Satan is also assaulting what you're going to do in heaven. Remember back in Chapter 8 that we discussed that we're forbidden from communicating with the dead. That goes both ways. So the dead are forbidden from communicating with us too. This reveals that you won't prey on the living like a zombie or vampire in the afterlife. Instead, one thing you'll do is pray for the living. The martyrs during the tribulation pray to God that he avenges their deaths (Revelation 6:9-10), all people in heaven pray (Revelation 5:8), and even Jesus himself prays for the living (Romans 8:34). You're also going to serve and help the living during Jesus's millennial reign on earth. After all, Jesus left heaven and came to earth to serve us (Mark 10:45). We're going to do the same when we return with him at his second coming. Remember that we're going to be rulers during that time (Matthew 25:23). You're going to be a doer for Jesus, using the unique skills he's given you to serve his kingdom and those living in it (1 Peter 4:10, James 1:22).

I'd like to point out a hidden truth about vampires. The way vampires are depicted in popular culture makes me think of fallen angels. Both are immortal, are trapped on the earth and unable to reach the afterlife, they prey on the living, they have beautiful bodies, they're afflicted by holy items, they're averse to the light, and they're intelligent. See how it's similar to the current life of a fallen angel?

Satan is indeed assaulting the afterlife through the popularity of the undead. Even though he makes it seem like he has the power over life and death and can usher in the undead apocalypse, you now know that God is the one who has all the power. As such, Satan and his fallen angels are doomed to the same fate as the undead zombies and vampires. A final demise. For the fallen angels, it's the lake of fire (Matthew 25:41).

You know, if you haven't yet put your faith in Jesus then you're walking dead. You're undead per se. That's because your destiny is currently the same as the fallen angels. It doesn't have to be. Choose Jesus and come back to life!

CHAPTER 12 – IT'S JUST A SIMULATION

Have you seen the movie *The Matrix* with Keanu Reeves?[1] Keanu plays the main character, Neo, who comes to realize he's living in a simulation run by machines which have taken over the planet. Or how about the new movie *Free Guy* with Ryan Reynolds?[2] Ryan plays the main character, Guy, who discovers that he's an NPC in a video game. An NPC is a non-player character. That means a person isn't controlling that avatar in the video game. Instead, the computer is. These popular movies are both about characters who live in a simulated reality and don't know it. Did you know that this is one of Satan's assaults on your afterlife?

There are some really smart people on the planet who think we're no different than Neo and Guy. They think we're living in a simulation too. That we're being controlled by aliens or an AI. On a podcast with Joe Rogan, Elon Musk said: "If you assume any rate of improvement at all, games will eventually be indistinguishable from reality...We're most likely in a simulation."[3] It's an idea gaining in popularity. Check out some of these headlines.

> "Elon Musk Says We May Live In A Simulation. Here's How We Might Tell If He's Right"[4]
> "Religion And The Simulation Hypothesis: Is God An AI (Part I)?"[5]
> "Are We Living In A Computer Simulation? I Don't Know. Probably."[6]
> "Do We Live In A Simulation? Chances Are About 50–50"[7]
> "15 Irrefutable Reasons Why We Might Be Living In A Simulation"[8]

It seems this hypothesis originated from an Oxford University philosopher, Nick Bostrom. In 2001, shortly after *The Matrix* came out, he wrote a simulation argument that postulates these scenarios: "(1) Humanity will go extinct before creating technology powerful enough to run convincing simulations of reality; (2) humanity will live to see such technology but decide, for whatever reason, not to run any simulations; (3) humanity will create that technology and run many different simulations of its evolutionary history — in which case there would be lots of simulated realities and only one non-simulated one, so maybe it's more likely than not that we're living in a simulation right now."[9]

So, it seems the reason people believe this is because we're now able to create video games and movies with graphics that look almost real. I watched some game footage of what many game websites are calling the most realistic game today. It's *Red Dead Redemption 2* if you want to have a look yourself.[10] I admit, it looks pretty real. Therefore, they reason we must be characters in one of these simulations.

Now, how they make the giant leap from our ability to create something to that means we must be living in that something, I honestly don't get. However, they say that us living in a simulation explains all sorts of odd things about our current existence, like the Mandela Effect. That's when a large number of people all have the same false memory. Here's a good example of that: What do you remember as the title of a popular children's book series, *The Berenstein Bears* or *The Berenstain Bears*? It's *The Berenstain Bears*, but a whole bunch of people remember it incorrectly.[11] Proponents of the simulation hypothesis say the Mandela Effect can be explained away because we live in a defective or buggy simulation.

A simulated reality also explains people who see apparitions. It's another bug. And some say the reason we haven't yet encountered aliens is because an advanced alien species is the one controlling our simulation and they're keeping their existence hidden from us. People are even using new scientific discoveries to support this simulation hypothesis. Scientists have been able to successfully store information directly onto our DNA.[12] So people extrapolate that to mean humans are just computer code at their most basic level.

People are using the simulation hypothesis to explain away reality, God, heaven, and hell. They say those are just constructs in the simulation, you see. It's become the latest theory of everything for an atheistic world. God's Word explains what's going on here. The apostle Paul told Timothy that in the last days there would be people who were forever learning, but never able to understand the truth (2 Timothy 3:1-7). God also says that the wisdom of the world is foolishness to God. That the wise are trapped in their own cleverness (1 Corinthians 3:19). That's exactly what the simulation hypothesis is, foolishness to God, and it has trapped people who are wise by the world's standards.

But we believers see right through this weapon of illusion created by Satan. That's because we have the mind of Christ (1 Corinthians 2:16) which enables us to understand the things of God and discern the truth. Instead of putting our faith in the wisdom of men, we trust in the power of God (1 Corinthians 2:5).

Are you seeing ways in which Satan's clever simulation idea is assaulting the afterlife? It's just like his first assault in the garden of Eden with Eve. He got Eve to question God and what he said (Genesis 3:1). Satan is doing the same thing here. "Did God say you aren't in a simulation?" "Did God say you aren't computer code?" "Did God say he isn't an AI?" Well, let's see what God actually said.

> For the wrath of God is revealed from heaven against all ungodliness and unrighteousness of men who suppress the truth in unrighteousness, because that which is known of God is revealed in them, for God revealed it to them. For the invisible things of him since the creation of the world are clearly seen, being perceived through the things that are made, even his everlasting power and divinity, that they may be without excuse. Because knowing God, they didn't glorify him as God, and didn't give thanks, but became vain in their reasoning, and their senseless heart was darkened. Professing themselves to be wise, they became fools, and traded the glory of the incorruptible God for the likeness of an image of corruptible man….
> … who exchanged the truth of God for a lie, and worshiped and served the creature rather than the Creator. (Romans 1:18-23, 25)

God has revealed the truth both in everyone and to everyone. Remember that he's written eternity into everyone's heart (Ecclesiastes 3:11). No one has an excuse for not knowing God. When people refuse to acknowledge God, they end up trading him for an image and then they worship that creation.

> "To an image carved from a piece of wood they say, 'You are my father.' To an idol chiseled from a block of stone they say, 'You are my mother.'" (Jeremiah 2:27 NLT)

> "What good is an idol carved by man, or a cast image that deceives you? How foolish to trust in your own creation—a god that can't even talk! What sorrow awaits you who say to wooden idols, 'Wake up and save us!'

Chapter 12 - It's Just A Simulation

> To speechless stone images you say, 'Rise up and teach us!' Can an idol tell you what to do? They may be overlaid with gold and silver, but they are lifeless inside." (Habakkuk 2:18-19 NLT)

Simulations run on computers. The brain of a computer is essentially the microprocessor. Do you know how a microprocessor is made? It's silicon, which comes from silica sand or quartz. Then all sorts of different metals like copper, aluminum, gold, and even hafnium, which is rarer than gold, are etched into it and layered onto it. The metals create the integrated circuits on the silicon wafer. At its most basic, it's just a stone decorated with gold and silver.

Do you see how the simulation hypothesis is just another idol, an image created by man and worshiped as God? We've created realistic video game worlds and now there are people who trust in those. It's trusting in our own creation, just like the Scripture says. The smart people behind this hypothesis are trusting in what they know how to create, which is computer code.

There's another Satanic assault on your afterlife with this simulation. There's no afterlife for you in this simulated reality. That's because you aren't a 'you' in this simulation of life. You're really just a bunch of ones and zeros. You aren't unique. You don't have any free will. You're just someone's puppet. A program that someone wrote. And when it comes time for your character to die, you just cease to exist. Your ones and zeros will just get deleted.

Hopefully, it's obvious to you that you are indeed a real person living on a very real planet earth that God created and is in control of. That reality doesn't cease to exist in the afterlife. It's going to be enhanced. You're going to have a new body that functions optimally (Philippians 3:21). All of your senses are going to be superior to what they are today. Remember that what we see and experience today is all under God's curse. When Jesus returns and sets up his kingdom, he's going to restore the earth (Isaiah 35, Revelation 22:3). We're going to get to see and experience the world in a whole new way.

You are still going to be you in heaven. You'll have a new body, but the same soul. Look at how many times "you" is used in this Scripture.

> Yet now he has reconciled you to himself through the death of Christ in his physical body. As a result, he has brought you into his own presence,

and you are holy and blameless as you stand before him without a single fault. (Colossians 1:22 NLT)

Whatever makes you unique, as long as it's not sinful, is going to remain with you in heaven. Do you love dogs, know how to speak ten languages, and enjoy cooking Mexican food? You're still going to love those things and get to do the things you enjoy in heaven. Did you know that languages, nations, and cultures all still exist in heaven? In this Scripture, the prophet Daniel has a vision of Jesus's second coming. Jesus is the "son of man."

> I saw in the night visions, and behold, there came with the clouds of the sky one like a son of man, and he came even to the Ancient of Days, and they brought him near before him. Dominion was given him, and glory, and a kingdom, that all the peoples, nations, and languages should serve him. His dominion is an everlasting dominion, which will not pass away, and his kingdom one that will not be destroyed. (Daniel 7:13-14)

In this description of Jesus's millennial reign on earth, which will be our future heaven, notice that it says all people, nations, and languages serve him. That means all those things and the good aspects about them will all be present. You're familiar with nations. You know that they have different languages, kinds of food, types of animals, languages, art, dance, music, and on it goes. Individual, unique people will make up those nations, just like today. Even after Jesus's millennial reign, when he creates a new earth and a new heaven, there will still be nations.

> The nations will walk in its light. The kings of the earth bring the glory and honor of the nations into it. (Revelation 21:24)

In fact, nations will bring their glory and honor to Jesus in the New Jerusalem. Just think of all the unique things that nations provide to rulers and dignitaries today. The National Archives website has pictures of gifts the President of the United States has received from other nations.[13] There are tea sets, paintings, sculptures, jewelry, and even pottery. You know, someone had to make each of those gifts. In the same way, unique someones will create the gifts that are brought to Jesus on the new earth.

Satan wants you to think that you're just like the character Guy in the movie, *Free Guy*. That you aren't unique and that you have a generic name. Well, one of the best things about the afterlife is names. It's why Satan assaults names. He blasphemes God's name (Revelation 13:6) when God's name is meant to be kept holy (Luke 11:2). It's because he knows there's power in Jesus's name (John 17:11). It's Jesus's name which saved you and keeps you.

Names are important to God. He let Adam name all the animals and birds and even Eve (Genesis 2:19-20, 3:20). He sent angels to tell people what to name their babies. That happened with Jesus (Matthew 1:21) and John the Baptist (Luke 1:13). He even renamed people. Abram became Abraham (Genesis 17:5), Sarai became Sarah (Genesis 17:15), Jacob became Israel (Genesis 32:28), and Simon became Peter (John 1:42). God did that because a name is an identity. God gives each of us a new identity when we place our faith in him. He doesn't obliterate our identity in the afterlife. He's going to give us a new one.

Each person who puts their faith in Jesus is going to get a "new name written" on a "white stone" when they get to heaven. It's going to be a unique and special name that's only between you and Jesus.

> "I will give him a white stone, and on the stone a new name written which no one knows but he who receives it." (Revelation 2:17)

> "I will in no way blot his name out of the book of life, and I will confess his name before my Father, and before his angels. ... I will write on him the name of my God and the name of the city of my God, the new Jerusalem, which comes down out of heaven from my God, and my own new name." (Revelation 3:5, 12)

Not only do you get a special new name in heaven, but you get God's name, Jesus's name, and the name of God's holy dwelling place all written onto you. It's no wonder Satan assaults your identity. All the things that Satan blasphemes about heaven are going to be written onto you.

You know how I mentioned earlier that scientists have figured out how to write information into our DNA? Well, God's been storing his truth in our DNA since creation. He's also recorded every day of our existence in his book (Psalm 139:16). God's Book of Life is something else Satan is assaulting with this simulation hypothesis. As a believer, your current name is written in Jesus's Book of Life. Satan wants to obliterate your name. To have it erased from Jesus's book so that you'll get sent to hell (Revelation 20:15). And just like Neo in *The Matrix* movie, Satan wants you to take the red pill and abort yourself from the simulation. But we're not in a simulation. So, you won't wake up in an earthly reality like Neo did. Taking a suicide pill will ensure you wake up in the afterlife. Don't swallow Satan's lie.

Satan is also trying to convince people that God's Book of Life means that you really are code and that you're just running out your programming per se. Well, you're not running on play. You have free will even though God already knows your fate (Isaiah 46:9-10). You know that you have free will because you make choices and think for yourself all the time. You can choose to put your faith in Jesus or not. We live inside a world that has time. God exists outside of that. He created time. He has a completely different view and perspective than we do. God knows all things—past, present, and future. Because he knows what's going to happen in the future, he can reveal it to us in the past. That's prophecy, predestination, or fate. To give an overly simplistic example, think of one of those books you read as a kid where you get to pick your own adventure. You know, where you decide what the character does in a situation and then flip to the corresponding next page. In that example, God is like the author, and you are like the reader. God wrote the story with every choice, adventure, and outcome accounted for and you get to choose which path you take.

There's one more promise about your name that I don't want you to miss in that Scripture above. Jesus is also going to announce your current name to God the Father and all the holy angels when he presents you. Perhaps a similar experience most of us have had is graduating from high school. The principle reads your name, you go up and get your diploma, and your family cheers and claps. Now, picture all the millions of holy angels cheering for you along with all your friends and family there. Instead of getting a diploma, you'll get a white stone with your new name. You can't tell me that isn't going to be awesome!

The simulation hypothesis is just that, a theory to explain away God and all his wonderful promises about the afterlife. I trust that you now see this illusion for what it really is, Satan's assault against your afterlife.

CHAPTER 13 - A MULTIVERSE OF DO-OVERS

In this assault on the afterlife, Satan is taking advantage of our desire for second chances and do-overs. We've all messed up or think we've missed out on something that we'd just like to do again. We repeat conversations in our mind and wish we'd said something different or better. So how would one go about doing life over? Enter time travel.

I'm sure you've wondered what you'd do differently in your life if you were able to travel back in time. Maybe you would have studied harder, taken a different job, moved somewhere exotic, married someone else, or taken better care of yourself. Or perhaps you'd travel back in time so that you could be with someone who's already died in the present day. There have been countless movies and books involving time travel and they just increase our appetite and longing to hit rewind on our lives. The *Back To The Future* movie franchise is a fond one of mine.[1]

Our fascination with this kind of science fiction drives our need to make it science fact. We can't help but pour our knowledge and ingenuity into figuring out how to make what seems impossible, possible. These headlines reveal that desire.

> "Paradox-Free Time Travel Is Theoretically Possible, Researchers Say"[2]
> "Time Travel Is Theoretically Possible, New Calculations Show. But That Doesn't Mean You Could Change The Past."[3]
> " 'We Can Build A Real Time Machine' "[4]
> "Time Travel: Five Ways That We Could Do It"[5]

Satan is happy to let us think that we can figure out how to control time and space. You see, if time travel were possible, then who would need an afterlife? You could live out an endless number of do-overs. Oh, and don't worry about getting old because if you could travel back in time, then why not travel forward when humanity has figured out how to live forever? Then once you've got your forever body you could travel to whenever and wherever you wanted. Now, the only problem is all the other people who will be traveling in time and messing up your do-over. You need a contained universe to do your time traveling in. One that no one could alter, but you. Enter the multiverse.

> "Why The Multiverse May Be The Most Dangerous Idea In Physics"[6]
> "This Is Why The Multiverse Must Exist"[7]
> "5 Reasons We May Live in a Multiverse"[8]
> "The Theory Of Parallel Universes Is Not Just Maths – It Is Science That Can Be Tested"[9]

What do you think of those headlines? The multiverse is a belief that there are multiple universes, parallel worlds, or alternate realities. The movie *Spider-Man: Into the Spider-Verse* depicts multiple parallel worlds in which each has a different Spider-Man.[10] This is time travel on a whole other level. Scientists already have multiple theories regarding how this could be possible. Some believe that because space is infinite and that there are only a finite number of ways in which particles can arrange themselves, that the particles will eventually repeat. So, beyond the farthest part of space that we can see might be another earth with another you. Or some believe there are places in the universe where cosmic inflation has stopped and created a bubble universe. So, there are multiple bubble universes. They also have theories supporting the possibility of a multiverse using quantum mechanics and string theory.[11] So now with this multiverse being a possibility, instead of traveling in time on the earth that you know, you could travel to an alternate reality where everything could be different and exciting.

Do you see the assault on the afterlife that's happening here? It's the modern-day version of reincarnation. Satan doesn't want you to know that there are no do-overs regarding salvation. After you die, your afterlife begins.

> It is appointed for men to die once, and after this, judgment. (Hebrews 9:27)

Satan also doesn't want you to know that time travel isn't possible. Just think about the possibility for a minute. Satan would have figured it out and would have been the first in line to use it.

> The wisdom we speak of is the mystery of God—his plan that was previously hidden, even though he made it for our ultimate glory before the world began. But the rulers of this world have not understood it; if they had, they would not have crucified our glorious Lord. (1 Corinthians 2:7-8 NLT)

God put his plan of salvation in place before the world began. "The rulers of this world" refers to Satan and his fallen angels. They didn't understand God's plan. They never would have let Jesus be crucified if they had. The crucifixion was their demise. They would do it over in a heartbeat. They haven't. Because they can't.

God created time. He created light, separated it from darkness, then evening passed and morning came, marking a day (Genesis 1:1-5). Since he created time, he's able to tell us the future. We believe God because what he reveals about the future always comes to pass.

> Remember the things I have done in the past. For I alone am God! I am God, and there is none like me. Only I can tell you the future before it even happens. Everything I plan will come to pass, for I do whatever I wish. (Isaiah 46:9-10 NLT)

Instead of hoping for endless do-overs, we must do what the apostle Paul did. He forgot the past and looked forward to the future, to heaven (Philippians 3:13-14). And speaking of heaven, there isn't a multiverse of afterlives, either. There's only one afterlife, and it lasts forever. Jesus died to give you eternal life (John 3:16). Gone forever will be every tear, sorrow, and pain (Revelation 21:4). However, if you choose not to accept Jesus, there's the eternal fire instead (Matthew 25:41).

I think one of the reasons we crave do-overs is because we have such a hard time being at peace. We can't let things go. We can't rest. We get anxious about every aspect of life and even the afterlife. We're constantly on the go and doing something. We think if we could just do this one thing perfect, then we'd be at peace. The trouble is that there's always another thing to get perfect. Satan doesn't have to push us into any of this, does he? But he'll certainly fan the flames of our unrest. He wants us to think we have to earn everything, including our salvation. Now, you already know that you can't. It's a gift from God that you can choose to accept or not (Romans 6:23).

While Jesus offers us peace right now by praying about everything (Philippians 4:6-7), it's sometimes difficult to attain, isn't it? It won't be that way in heaven. It's a place of eternal peace and rest. Here's a description about Jesus's millennial kingdom.

> The LORD will mediate between peoples and will settle disputes between strong nations far away. They will hammer their swords into plowshares and their spears into pruning hooks. Nation will no longer fight against nation, nor train for war anymore. Everyone will live in peace and prosperity, enjoying their own grapevines and fig trees, for there will be nothing to fear. The LORD of Heaven's Armies has made this promise! (Micah 4:3-4 NLT)

When Jesus returns at his second coming, he's going to establish his kingdom and reign from Jerusalem. "Everyone will live in peace." Peace on earth isn't a fantasy. It's going to happen in the not-too-distant future. Now, you might be thinking this is just a thousand years. What happens afterwards on the new earth? God's Word tells us that Jesus's kingdom and peace will never end (Isaiah 9:6-7). Jesus promises us rest for our weary souls (Matthew 11:28-29).

Perhaps all this talk about eternity in heaven being peaceful has made you anxious because now you think it'll be boring. There's Satan's assault on your afterlife again. God tells us that we'll experience pleasures forever (Psalm 16:11). Boredom isn't fun and doesn't bring pleasure. So, it's not going to exist in heaven. What will exist in heaven is all the fruits of the Spirit: love, joy, peace, patience, kindness, goodness, faith, gentleness, and self-control (Galatians 5:22-23). Think about all the wonderful times that await you.

You don't need to worry about second chances, regrets, and do-overs. You're going to live forever. You'll be able to do things that you never got a chance to do or that you messed up at. You know, I was a musician when I was younger. I played the oboe and was good enough to audition for the city junior symphony when I was eleven. I missed it by one chair. So, you know what I did? I quit playing. Yep. What can I say? I was only eleven. I sometimes wonder what might have happened if I hadn't. While I could stress out about how I could learn it over again and resume playing today, I know that I'll have all the time in the world to do it in heaven, if I want to. Not only that, but I'll also have the best musicians throughout time that chose to put their faith in Jesus to help me learn it again.

Maybe you're worried about who you'll be with in heaven because you regret your marriage choice or choices. Or perhaps you're single and are afraid you'll be alone for forever. Jesus was asked about marriage in heaven. He said that we aren't married or given in marriage in heaven and that we'll be like the angels (Matthew 22:30). The apostle Paul described this as a great mystery but said it's because we'll already be married to Jesus (Ephesians 5:31-32). The church, that's us believers, and Jesus are one. However, this doesn't mean you'll be alone. God knows that it's not good for man to be alone (Genesis 2:18). That's why he made Eve for Adam. You're going to have plenty of fulfilling relationships of all kinds in heaven. There will be people as close to you as a spouse is. You'll have best friends, sisters, brothers, aunts, uncles, and even parent figures.

What about kids you say? Well, the Bible doesn't say that babies and children who die are suddenly all grown up in heaven. So, I imagine there will be all sorts of children who get to grow up in heaven that you'll get to be with. If you aren't a fan of children today because they're loud, don't listen, and are often naughty, then rest assured that they won't be sinners in heaven. And we shouldn't forget about the millennial reign with Jesus. It's going to have a mix of immortal believers and regular non-immortal humans. It starts out with the people who survived the tribulation and also put their faith in Jesus. They're going to start families. So, there will be successive generations of people. There will be plenty of babies and children in the millennial kingdom who need watching, caring, coaching, and even teaching.

Don't let Satan assault your afterlife with his lies about time travel and his multiverse of do-overs. You're going to have an infinite number of second chances in heaven. Trust that your eternal future is safe in the hands of Jesus.

> Jesus, crying with a loud voice, said, "Father, into your hands I commit my spirit!" (Luke 23:46)

CHAPTER 14 - EVOLVE INTO A TRANSHUMAN

Evolution. The belief that creation evolved from space sludge by accident. That humans are descendants of apes. It's Satan's assault on everything about God. God's existence, God's creation, our humanity, how we're made in the image of God, how God is in control, etc. That lie has worked so well that Satan has come up with a new evolution to assault the afterlife with. It's called transhumanism.

Transhumans believe that aging is a disease and that being human isn't the final stage of our species' evolution.[1] They pursue this evolution through technology and science. Think human-computer interactions and genetic engineering. Technology like Elon Musk's Neuralink, the chip that goes into your brain and enables you to communicate with technology directly with your brain.[2] It's nanobots, you know, microscopic robots, that can be injected into your body to repair cells and cure disease. It's designing humans using genetic engineering. Want an extra arm or eyes like an eagle? The technology exists to make it happen. Cloning also fits in this space. They're cloning organs for transplants. It doesn't stop there, though. They'd like to clone your body and transfer your consciousness to a new, younger you. And if they can clone you, that means they could resurrect the dead with just some of their DNA. Yet who needs a body of flesh when you could be an android instead? But bodies that can live forever isn't their ultimate goal. A life without a body, as a digital avatar, in a simulated environment or reality is where this evolution is headed. Since this life extending and human transforming technology is still in development and testing, there's also cryogenics. Bodies can be stored in a super cold environment and then thawed sometime in the future when they can be brought back to life.[3]

You know, there are some things about the advancements we're making in technology and science that are really cool. Have you started thinking about what you'd change about yourself or augment yourself with? I'm thinking of Inspector Gadget.[4] Do you remember that cartoon? Gadget was a transhuman, part man and part machine and had all sorts of crazy tech that augmented him. I could see myself clicking a button on my wrist, a helicopter propeller coming out of my arm, and me flying away. Am I sinful because I think that'd be cool?

Well, we shouldn't desire to alter or augment what God has created and deemed very good. When we go down that path, we start to put ourselves in the place of God, creating things that God told us not to. Things like idols that we end up worshiping, or new animals and plants that we've mixed together traits from different species. Before long, we've completely corrupted God's creation. All because we decided to play God.

The technology and the science advancements aren't necessarily evil in and of themselves. It's what we do with them that makes them evil. If that helicopter gadget just attached to me like a bracelet, instead of actually being part of me, it would be different. It wouldn't be corrupting God's creation as a bracelet. It wouldn't be assaulting God's image and how he made me in that image. So, we have to be really careful with how we use what we're inventing because it can easily become a weapon used by Satan in his assault on the afterlife.

I know this all sounds very much like science fiction. If you're not aware of these things, you need to know that the technobillionaires on the planet are putting a lot of their money, time, and resources into this. Since humans haven't evolved into some other species yet, the technocrats have decided to pursue a man-made evolution instead. You'd think that humanity actually degrading and not improving or evolving over time would be enough to debunk evolution. Yet here we are. See for yourself with these headlines.

> "Elon Musk: Humans Must Merge With Machines Or Become Irrelevant In AI Age"[5]
> "Human Immortality: Will Harvard's Genetic Reset Trials Help Us Live Forever?"[6]
> "New Blood, Computer Brains And Frozen Heads: How Billionaires 'Will Live Forever'"[7]
> "Peter The Human Cyborg's Mind-Blowing Journey To 'Cheat Death' As Part Man, Part Machine"[8]
> "Transhumanism: The New Religion Of The Coming Technocracy"[9]
> "Elon Musk Mocks Jeff Bezos' Attempt to Develop Immortality Tech"[10]

It makes me really sad when I read some articles and research about transhumanism. Some have a desire to replace what God created with something man-made. For some reason they believe the man-made item is superior, better engineered, and won't break down. Now, I can't think of a single mechanical item that lasts longer than a body. Can you? Vehicles quit working, need constant maintenance, and eventually rust and fall apart. Computer hard drives don't even last as long as a vehicle. They malfunction, freeze, run out of space, and stop working in often times just a couple years. And they need constant maintenance too. Think of all the viruses that attack everything technology today. Cyber warfare isn't going to go away if everyone is part human and part machine. It'll just get way worse. A nation could eradicate an entire army with a computer virus instead of using conventional and bio weapons.

I can think of countless practical issues with transhumanism. I mean what happens if you need to charge your artificial limbs and the power goes out and you can't do solar power because it's nighttime? What if someone hacks your brain chip and implants false memories? What if the nanobots malfunction and kill cells instead of repairing them? Can nanobots be hacked and reprogrammed? Will genetically altering your eyes for eagle vision unknowingly impact your ability to fight off certain diseases? If you get an organ transplant that was grown in a pig will that give you pig DNA? See what I mean? I'm sure you can think of all sorts of problems too.

So, what's going on here? If it's obvious to us that this is a flawed pursuit, why is it being so heavily invested in and sought after? God's Word says, "professing themselves to be wise, they became fools."

> For the wrath of God is revealed from heaven against all ungodliness and unrighteousness of men who suppress the truth in unrighteousness, because that which is known of God is revealed in them, for God revealed it to them. For the invisible things of him since the creation of the world are clearly seen, being perceived through the things that are made, even his everlasting power and divinity, that they may be without excuse. Because knowing God, they didn't glorify him as God, and didn't give thanks, but became vain in their reasoning, and their senseless heart was darkened. Professing themselves to be wise, they became fools.... ... Even as they refused to have God in their knowledge, God gave them up to a reprobate mind, to do those things which are not fitting; ... hateful to God, insolent,

arrogant, boastful, inventors of evil things. (Romans 1:18-22, 28, 30)

We talked about the "reprobate" mind in a prior chapter. It's the mind that Satan has. It literally can't think clearly. It's insanity. People with this kind of mind do things and pursue things that "are not fitting." Since they hate God and are arrogant, they become "inventors of evil things."

Let's examine how Satan is using this evil thing called a transhuman to assault the afterlife. First, there's a clear assault on the existence of the afterlife. According to the philosophy of transhumanism on humanityplus.org, they aren't afraid of death because they believe it's just the end of existence.[11] They want to prolong life because they want to keep living, experiencing, creating, etc.

We know the afterlife exists because Jesus rose from the dead! It wasn't a secret. He was seen by hundreds of eyewitnesses (1 Corinthians 15). Furthermore, that Scripture we read above makes it clear that God has revealed his truth to everyone. No one will have the excuse that they didn't know that God or the afterlife existed. This just reveals the second assault on the afterlife, an attempt to escape God's judgment.

To anyone who's watching for Jesus's return, it's obvious it could happen any minute. Just like in Noah's day, people are ignoring and scoffing at the warnings. Since no one has an excuse to deny God's existence, it means they're ignoring his existence. People don't want to think about God or the afterlife. People are choosing to disregard that it's God who decides how long each person lives (Job 14:5). They want to decide for themselves how long to live because they want to live life large. It's this you only live once mentality. Because they've chosen not to get to know God, they believe all the lies Satan has told them. That God is boring. That being a Christian is no fun.

I think back to Noah's day because Jesus said it would be like those days when he returns (Matthew 24:37). The *Ancient Book of Jasher* provides some interesting detail about what happened when the flood came.[12]

> And all the fountains of the deep were broken up, and the windows of heaven were opened, and the rain was upon the earth forty days and forty nights. And Noah and his household, and all the living creatures that were

with him, came into the ark on account of the waters of the flood, and the Lord shut him in. And all the sons of men that were left upon the earth, became exhausted through evil on account of the rain, for the waters were coming more violently upon the earth, and the animals and beasts were still surrounding the ark. And the sons of men assembled together, about seven hundred thousand men and women, and they came unto Noah to the ark. And they called to Noah, saying, Open for us that we may come to thee in the ark—and wherefore shall we die? And Noah, with a loud voice, answered them from the ark, saying, Have you not all rebelled against the Lord, and said that he does not exist? and therefore the Lord brought upon you this evil, to destroy and cut you off from the face of the earth. Is not this the thing that I spoke to you of one hundred and twenty years back, and you would not hearken to the voice of the Lord, and now do you desire to live upon earth? And they said to Noah, We are ready to return to the Lord; only open for us that we may live and not die. And Noah answered them, saying, Behold now that you see the trouble of your souls, you wish to return to the Lord; why did you not return during these hundred and twenty years, which the Lord granted you as the determined period? But now you come and tell me this on account of the troubles of your souls, now also the Lord will not listen to you, neither will he give ear to you on this day, so that you will not now succeed in your wishes. (Ancient Book of Jasher, chapter 6:14-23)

Noah preached for 120 years about God's coming judgment and the need to repent and turn to him. No one listened to him. They didn't believe him. When the flood came and they all came against the ark, Noah tells us the people had "rebelled against the Lord" and said, "he does not exist." A bit later we see the truth of what they really believed. They told Noah "we are ready to return to the Lord." Oh, so they really did know that God existed. They just didn't want to obey him. They were ignoring the warnings of his coming judgment. They figured they could escape God's judgment at the last second. They weren't saved because they never repented and truly opened their hearts to let God in. They just didn't want to die. This same thing is happening today with transhumanism.

The third transhuman assault on your afterlife is Satan's lie that you need to enhance your body because it's flawed and poorly designed. The reason our bodies age, get diseased, break, and eventually die is because of the curse (Genesis 3, Romans 8:18-23). When Adam and Eve sinned, it resulted in death and decay. The consequence of sin is death (Romans 6:23). But Jesus conquered death!

> But when this perishable body will have become imperishable, and this mortal will have put on immortality, then what is written will happen: "Death is swallowed up in victory. Death, where is your sting? Hades, where is your victory?" The sting of death is sin, and the power of sin is the law. But thanks be to God, who gives us the victory through our Lord Jesus Christ. (1 Corinthians 15:54-57)

In heaven you're going to have a perfect immortal body. It won't be flawed. It will be indestructible. It won't need any repair or regular maintenance. Consider this. The people who lived prior to the flood lived a really long time. Adam was 930 years old, Noah was 950 years old, and Methuselah was the oldest human ever at 969 years old (Genesis 5:5, 27, 9:29). And they didn't even have immortal super bodies yet! Even people after the flood lived a long time for many generations. Abraham was 175 years old, and Moses was 120 years old (Genesis 25:7, Deuteronomy 34:7). God knows how to make a body that lasts.

We're promised an immortal body that's like Jesus's resurrected body (Philippians 3:21, 1 John 3:2). Jesus could do some pretty cool things with his body. He could materialize places (John 20:19) and he could disappear (Luke 24:31). I'm totally convinced we're going to be able to teleport. Jesus teleported Philip (Acts 8:39-40). And it seems Elijah was teleported often by God since the prophets assumed God had dropped him off in a valley somewhere when he was raptured (2 Kings 2:16). Jesus floated on clouds (Acts 1:9). You know he walked on water and so did Peter (Matthew 14:25-29). We're going to shine (Matthew 13:43, Daniel 12:3). Don't think glow-in-the-dark like a jellyfish. It's more like you're going to reflect God's glory and radiate. Remember Moses's face had a radiant glow after he'd been on the mountain with God for 40 days (Exodus 34:29-35). You're also going to see everything with perfect clarity and will know fully (1 Corinthians 13:12). This implies our senses will be perfect. While we won't be all-knowing because that's God, it means we'll understand fully. There won't be any difficulty with learning and certainly no deception. Only truth.

The last way that Satan is assaulting the afterlife through transhumanism is with *extropia*. It was a new word to me too. Transhumanists have coined the term to mean a never-ending movement, a state of perpetual progress. They reject utopia because they say it's static.[13] And there you have the blow from Satan. It's his lie that heaven is boring, stale, never changing, and old. He doesn't need to come up with new lies, he just recycles and repackages them. In the last chapter we discussed that the lack of God's peace leads to a hamster on a wheel type of life in which you're constantly running, never achieving, and craving endless do-overs. It's a restless state of existence. God's peace and rest that he promises in the afterlife doesn't mean doing nothing. Death isn't the end of living, experiencing, exploring, creating, or learning if your destination is heaven. We're going to be active in heaven, but never tired or exhausted.

There's an important truth about heaven in this Scripture. God is the one "who sits on the throne." God says this when he makes the new earth and new heaven. It's the word *making*.

> He who sits on the throne said, "Behold, I am making all things new." (Revelation 21:5)

Making is an active tense. It means that it's ongoing. It doesn't say made. That would mean it was finished. No. It says making. That's not static at all, is it? God isn't static. That would mean that he's finite. God is infinite and has no limits (Psalm 147:5, Psalm 139). He loves to make new things and do new things (Isaiah 43:18-19). He is a creator (Genesis 1:1). He never changes (Malachi 3:6). So that means he's always going to be creating. Your utopia isn't going to be static.

You don't need to evolve into a new species, a transhuman, in order to live forever. You just need to put your faith in Jesus and then let him transform you into his glorious image (2 Corinthians 3:18).

I mentioned earlier that the transhumanist evolution is headed toward a life without a body, as a digital avatar. Join me in the next chapter as we unpack Satan's lie about achieving immortality as a posthuman.

CHAPTER 15 - ACHIEVE IMMORTALITY AS A POSTHUMAN

As we continue down the transhuman evolutionary path, I was reading about another cool thing that many of the big tech companies are creating. It's called a metaverse. Facebook is working on one. So is Microsoft. Think of the metaverse as a digital world that you could do life in. If you've read the book or seen the movie *Ready Player One*, OASIS is a metaverse.[1] The main character, Wade, spent most of his time in the digital world, OASIS. He had a 3D avatar that could interact with other people and objects. He hung out with friends, played games, danced, and drove a car. It was life in a virtual world. If you're a gamer and like to play virtual reality games, the game worlds you play in are a metaverse.

Here's how Mark Zuckerberg described the metaverse that Facebook is building in a recent phone interview with a reporter at The Verge: "You can think about the metaverse as an embodied internet, where instead of just viewing content — you are in it. And you feel present with other people as if you were in other places, having different experiences that you couldn't necessarily do on a 2D app or webpage, like dancing, for example, or different types of fitness. ... If you want to talk to someone, you're working through a problem, instead of just calling them on the phone, they can teleport in, and then they can see all the context that you have. They can see your five monitors, or whatever it is, and the documents or all the windows of code that you have, or a 3D model that you're working on. And they can stand next to you and interact, and then in a blink they can teleport back to where they were and kind of be in a separate place. ... In the future, instead of just doing this over a phone call, you'll be able to sit as a hologram on my couch, or I'll be able to sit as a hologram on your couch, and it'll actually feel like we're in the same place, even if we're in different states or hundreds of miles apart."[2]

Okay, you can't tell me that doesn't sound cool. I mean come on, wouldn't you like to teleport somewhere virtually? I could see myself walking through a museum in a foreign country, virtually. I can envision myself attending a concert or sporting event virtually with my friends and family all next to me.

The possibilities for the metaverse are enormous. It's going to drive an entirely new economy. That museum I want to walk through could be filled with art that's only found in the multiverse. Virtual museums would pay artists to create digital art. Museums could charge people admission. You could even have your own house in a metaverse that you design however you want and then fill it with whatever you buy in the metaverse. Yes, you could certainly own items in the metaverse. That tech is already being used today. Perhaps you've heard of NFTs?[3] Those are non-fungible tokens. Meaning they are unique tokens which are stored on a blockchain, which is the foundation of crypto currency. Since it's unique, that means only one person could own the digital version. So, you can interact, do things, own stuff, and even work in the metaverse. Do you see how the metaverse could be like a city?

We have to remember that Satan likes to put evil weapons in really cool packages. A key problem with the metaverse is that it's conditioning us to accept and even desire life in a virtual world. Life in a world that we humans created, not the world that God created for us. It's assaulting everything physical, everything that God created. This conditioning is necessary to achieve the end goal of the transhumanist evolution. The posthuman. Here's how humanityplus.org describes that state of being: "exceeding the limitations that define the less desirable aspects of the 'human condition.' ... Posthuman beings would no longer suffer from disease, aging and inevitable death ... They would have vastly greater physical capability and freedom of form ... Posthumans would also have much greater cognitive capabilities, and more refined emotions."[4] The posthuman isn't human at all. It's humans becoming digital and living forever in a digital reality.

Why do you think there are companies like Elon Musk's Neuralink working on brain to computer interfaces? It's because they want to upload a brain, a consciousness they say, to a computer. That digital consciousness would then live in a virtual environment. A human constructed heaven made of ones and zeros.

Amazon even has a new TV show about this. It's called *Upload*.[5] The main character is on the verge of death and chooses to be uploaded into a virtual heaven. Uploads get to pick which heaven they want to live in. Like a tropical paradise or a city. Of course, none of the heavens are free. The uploads can even communicate with people who haven't died and been uploaded. Living people just appear as a hologram in the virtual heaven. A downside for living people is that they're expected to support and provide for uploads because uploads can run out of digital currency and even data. Yes, data. You see, it takes a lot of bandwidth to live in a virtual world.

Can you see how much Satan hates God and everything that God created, including you? He is bombarding us with this simulation lie. He wants us to believe we either already live in a simulation or that we're meant to live in one of our own making in the future, permanently. And the billionaires on the planet are totally bought in. Check out these headlines.

> "Elon Musk's Big Neuralink Paper: Should We Prepare For The Digital Afterlife?"[6]
> "Life After Death: Physicist Michio Kaku Says Digital Immortality Is 'Within Reach' "[7]
> "Deepak Chopra And Richard Branson To Live On Forever Through AI, Here's How"[8]
> "Could AI Keep People 'Alive' After Death?"[9]
> "The Digital Afterlife Is Open For Business. But It Needs Rules."[10]

Smart people believe Satan's lie about the afterlife being digital because they want to construct their own heaven, their own afterlife. They're full of pride, just like Satan. While many of these people claim to be atheists, their actions betray them. Their desire to live forever in an afterlife is proof that God put a desire for eternity into their hearts. Otherwise, wouldn't they be okay with just living and dying? This digital afterlife is also a mechanism to escape. I think that's one of the main draws of the metaverse. It's a way to escape what's going on in the world. The digital afterlife is their way to escape both the world, which they view as dismal, and God's judgment.

This same sort of thing happened before in history, shortly after the flood. God told Noah and his family to be fruitful, multiply, and fill the earth (Genesis 9:1). However, that's not what most of his descendants chose to do. Instead, they all got together and built a city. The Tower of Babel was in that city (Genesis 11). You see, they wanted to make a name for themselves, and they wanted to escape any future judgment. That's why the tower was constructed waterproof, with tar, and reached into the heavens. It was going to be their haven if God flooded the earth again. But it was even more than that, they also had an evil desire to conquer heaven and take over.

Do you see the similarity to today with our desire to build a digital city for the afterlife? In both cases, man is placing himself above God. We've made the afterlife about our will, our desire, and our glory. Just like the Tower of Babel. But it's supposed to be about God's will and God's desire (Matthew 6:10). He's the only one who deserves the glory (Revelation 4:11).

Now, as for escaping judgment, you already know that there's no hiding from God. He's everywhere and sees everything (Psalm 139:7-12). When you die, you immediately start your afterlife (Hebrews 9:27). Satan wants you to think that God has totally messed up the afterlife and that it's just horrible. So, you need to escape God's design and live in your own. His lie about making your own heaven is a deception that will indeed get you an afterlife that's horrible. It's the same eternity that Satan is getting, hell. We needn't have any fear about the afterlife not meeting our expectations. God isn't going to trick us. He knows how to give good gifts (Matthew 7:9-11). Heaven is going to be way better than what you currently experience on earth.

> Now we live with great expectation, and we have a priceless inheritance—an inheritance that is kept in heaven for you, pure and undefiled, beyond the reach of change and decay. ... So be truly glad. There is wonderful joy ahead, even though you have to endure many trials for a little while. These trials will show that your faith is genuine. It is being tested as fire tests and purifies gold—though your faith is far more precious than mere gold. So when your faith remains strong through many trials, it will bring you much praise and glory and honor on the day when Jesus Christ is revealed to the whole world. You love him even though you have never seen him. Though you do not see him now, you trust him; and you rejoice with a glorious, inexpressible joy. ... It is all so wonderful that even the angels are eagerly watching these things happen. (1 Peter 1:3-4, 6-8, 12 NLT)

I love this Scripture because I can't help but smile when I read it. Especially the last verse. The holy angels are watching everything in eager anticipation. They can't wait for us to see what God's preparing for us. They can't wait to meet us. They can't wait to see who gets saved today and places their faith in Jesus. They throw a party every time it happens (Luke 15:10). If the angels who live in heaven, in God's very presence, are excited for us, shouldn't we be excited ourselves? There's going to be so much joy that Peter said it's "inexpressible." Jesus said if we put our faith in him and walk closely with him, then our desires would align with his. That's when we're able to ask for anything we desire and we'll get it (John 15:7). You're going to be abiding with Jesus when you get to heaven. Trust that your desires are going to be met. God's got this!

Now, we've already tackled some of the obvious assaults on the afterlife that posthumanism represents in prior chapters. Heaven and hell are both real, physical places. You're going to have a real, physical, immortal, super body in the afterlife. You're not a bunch of ones and zeros. God created you as a unique individual and he's even going to present you with a new name in heaven.

So, let's discuss a new weapon that Satan is wielding in this posthuman assault. Scientists are making the assumption that the information they upload or transfer from someone's brain to the computerized afterlife is their consciousness. They're equating information with life. Here's a good example. If you've seen the Marvel movies, you'll remember J.A.R.V.I.S.[11] He started out as Tony Stark's computer in *Iron Man*. He was an AI. Well, he eventually got an android body and became an Avenger. He was treated like a human, and in the comics even got married and had children. So, since we can have something that was digital become human, that must mean that humans can become digital. The problem is that your soul is not information that's stored in your brain. Your soul is separate from your body. You are body, soul, and spirit (1 Thessalonians 5:23). And we also know that a body without a spirit is dead (James 2:26). The only spirit who can give life to a body is God's Spirit (1 Corinthians 2:12, Hebrews 2:14-15). You know full well that God's life-giving Spirit, his breath of life, is not in any machine. However real it may act, a digital upload isn't real. It's just another AI.

The last assault against your afterlife that I'd like to address with posthumanism is Satan's temptation of freedom. One of the reasons I think the metaverse that Facebook is creating is cool is because of the freedom it'll provide. Today, there are several things that limit my ability to travel to a tourist attraction in another country. If I want to visit the Louvre Museum in Paris, France it would cost quite a bit of money to fly there, stay in a hotel, and live in the city for a few days. It would also take a lot of time to get there, stay there, and come back. Now, if I could just put on a virtual reality headset and visit the Louvre Museum from the comfort of my sofa one Saturday afternoon, there's a lot of freedom in that, isn't there? Many people think that heaven has limitations similar to what we have to deal with on earth today. It's Satan's lie that heaven is bureaucratic and a place where it's difficult to do things. That is such a lie! Heaven is the place of ultimate freedom. It's limitless.

Jesus is the one speaking in this verse. "The thief" is a reference to Satan. Jesus promises abundant life.

> The thief comes only in order to steal and kill and destroy. I came that they may have and enjoy life, and have it in abundance [to the full, till it overflows]. (John 10:10, AMP)

And you'll notice that Jesus's promise of abundant life means overflowing. Everything about life in heaven is going to overflow.

Are you limited financially today? In heaven you won't be. As a believer, you're a child of God (Romans 8:14-17). A co-heir of all that there is to inherit. You're going to have treasure and rewards in heaven (Luke 12:33-34). You won't need to earn a living in order to support yourself. God is going to freely provide for you from his own house (Psalm 36:8-9). You're going to have a home that Jesus is preparing just for you (John 14:2-3). You don't have to pay for it. It's a gift. All of heaven is a gift for you!

Are you limited physically today? Maybe that's why the metaverse and a posthuman world are appealing to you. You could dance or go fly fishing and you just can't physically do those things today. In heaven you won't be limited. You're getting a new body that'll be immortal and work perfectly (1 Corinthians 15:53). We're even going to be able to overcome the limits of physics that we have today. Peter walked on water with Jesus's help (Matthew 14:25-29) and Philip got teleported (Acts 8:39-40). Your forever body isn't going to have the limits that your earthly body does. You won't need a metaverse or digital heaven to travel to wherever you want to go. You won't need a virtual reality headset to participate in any activity that you can't do in real life today.

Are you limited because of a lack of relationships today? Maybe you're lonely and don't have anyone to do things with. In heaven, you're going to have a bunch of friends. Anyone you've ever helped in some way who makes it into heaven is going to welcome you into their heavenly home (Luke 16:9). And this isn't just referring to people you've directly helped. It's anyone you've indirectly helped and are likely not even aware of helping too. If you've donated to your church, a food bank, a clothing drive, or even prayed for strangers you don't know, all of those things have indirectly helped someone. Jesus will also be your friend (John 15:14-15). And we mustn't forget about the holy angels. They're going to enjoy our hospitality in heaven (Hebrews 13:2) and will also continue ministering to us in heaven (Hebrews 1:14).

Are you limited by fear and anxiety today? Perhaps you can't visit the Louvre Museum today because you're afraid of flying. That's why the metaverse and the digital afterlife are tempting. Here's some great news for you. There is absolutely no fear in heaven! You're going to be fearless.

> God is love, and he who remains in love remains in God, and God remains in him. In this, love has been made perfect among us, that we may have boldness in the day of judgment, because as he is, even so we are in this world. There is no fear in love; but perfect love casts out fear, because fear has punishment. He who fears is not made perfect in love. (1 John 4:16-18)

"There is no fear in love." Heaven is love because it's where God dwells and "God is love." You won't have any fear of punishment or of not being good enough in heaven because you will have overcome it by putting your faith in Jesus. You won't have any fear of pain because that doesn't exist in heaven either (Revelation 21:4).

Are you limited because of your job, career, or a life circumstance today? Perhaps you're liking this fake digital afterlife because you'd get to be anything you want in the afterlife. Maybe you've had a longing to be a teacher, but you just haven't been able to go to school and get the education you need for that career. Well, God is going to give you things to do in heaven that he literally created you for (1 Peter 4:10, Ephesians 2:10). There will be many opportunities for you to teach fellow immortal believers in heaven and even people who survive the tribulation and live out their lives during the millennial reign of Jesus.

Whatever it is that limits you today that makes a posthuman existence appealing, that limit will vanish in heaven.

> He who didn't spare his own Son, but delivered him up for us all, how would he not also with him freely give us all things? (Romans 8:32)

God's promise is that he will "freely give us all things." What things? All things! Anything you can think of. Of course, that's anything not sinful because there's no sin in heaven. A body that doesn't hurt, a pet, a fulfilling mission, food, a friend, clothing, a vacation, etc. And do they have a cost? No, they're free! So don't believe Satan's lie that you need to be a posthuman in order to live life large and limitless. Heaven is the place of ultimate freedom and abundance.

CHAPTER 16 - BE MORE THAN HUMAN AS A HYBRID

This particular Satanic assault on the afterlife is something Jesus told us would surface in the end times, right before his second coming. Jesus said it would be like it was during the days of Noah when he returns (Matthew 24:37). We briefly discussed what happened then back in Chapter 2.2.

Some fallen angels married human women and had giant children who were human-angel hybrids, the Nephilim (Genesis 6:1-12). At some point the earth became completely corrupted because the fallen angels polluted the human gene pool. You see, other than being jealous of human relationships, the fallen angels ultimately wanted to keep mankind out of heaven and kick God out of heaven. Satan didn't want the prophesied savior, Jesus, to ever be born of the woman (Genesis 3:15). Remember that God told Satan that the woman's seed would strike his head, kill him. So, if Satan could ensure that there weren't any humans anymore, well that would ruin God's plan, wouldn't it? Noah and his family were the only uncorrupted, pure humans left on the planet who worshiped God. That's why God saved them. Did you know that Noah preached for 120 years that God was going to destroy the earth and people needed to repent and turn to him (Genesis 6:3)? No one else got saved. God's judgment came and all the Nephilim and any unbelieving humans died in the flood. If you want to learn more about the Nephilim, I recommend you read *Judgment of the Nephilim* by Ryan Pitterson.[1]

Now, we can't just blame the fallen angels for what happened. Women were clearly involved as the other party in the hybrid baby making. Their fathers and brothers were involved too, giving them over in marriage to a fallen angel. People knew what they were doing, and they were okay with it. And after people saw that human-angel hybrids who were giant and strong were a result, I imagine the angels and hybrids became even more desirable than plain old humans. People in Noah's day wanted to be more than human. They wanted to be hybrids.

I think this assault is one of Satan's favorites because he repeats it. Since his plan didn't work prior to the flood, he tried it again afterward!

Satan wasn't thrilled with God's flood reboot, so he convinced another set of fallen angels to commit that same sin again after the flood. Whether they slept with human women again or used some kind of genetic engineering, we don't know. In any case, giants inhabited the entire promised land before the Israelites moved in (Numbers 13:27-33). Remember, David and the giant Goliath (1 Samuel 17)? So yet again, there were people who desired to be more than human. God even gave the Israelites this law so they would know his position on creating hybrids.

> " 'You shall not cross-breed different kinds of animals. You shall not sow your field with two kinds of seed.' " (Leviticus 19:19)

Do you recall what happened to all the post-flood giants? All of the giants conveniently decided to live on the land that God promised to Abraham and his descendants for forever. This was Satan's assault on the afterlife. He wanted to prevent the Israelites from attaining their forever land, their heaven on earth. God instructed the Israelites to conquer the promised land and to kill all of the inhabitants (1 Chronicles 20:8, Deuteronomy 1:19-30). God said he would be with them like he was in Egypt against Pharoah. Eventually, all of the giants were destroyed.

Why was God set on destroying these people, but not others? Why didn't God tell the Israelites to live with the giants, to teach the giants God's law, and to help the giants learn how to obey God? After all, foreigners were living among the Israelites worshiping God (Numbers 15:15). It's because the foreigners living in the promised land were very different. They were giants. Hybrids. It's because they aren't eligible for God's gift of salvation!

Jesus doesn't offer redemption to the immortal angels. He doesn't offer redemption to human-angel hybrids, either. Jesus, "the Son," only offers salvation to humans, the "descendants of Abraham." Don't worry, as a believer, God considers you a descendant of Abraham. It's not about being an actual descendant of his (Romans 9:6-8). The Bible clarifies that the children of Abraham are those who put their faith in Jesus (Galatians 3:7).

> Because God's children are human beings—made of flesh and blood—the

> Son also became flesh and blood. For only as a human being could he die, and only by dying could he break the power of the devil, who had the power of death. Only in this way could he set free all who have lived their lives as slaves to the fear of dying. We also know that the Son did not come to help angels; he came to help the descendants of Abraham. Therefore, it was necessary for him to be made in every respect like us, his brothers and sisters, so that he could be our merciful and faithful High Priest before God. Then he could offer a sacrifice that would take away the sins of the people. (Hebrews 2:14-17 NLT)

Don't you think it's quite interesting and revealing that this Scripture above, about salvation being only for humans, is even in the Bible? It seems like it would be meant for angels and not us. Yet there it is, in our Bible. There's a reason God has to tell us that being a human is required for his salvation. And specifically, that angels are excluded from it. I think it's because God knows we're going to be tempted into becoming something that we aren't meant to be, like an angel.

Back in Chapter 11 when we talked about the undead, you learned that people are body, soul, and spirit. Either you have the Holy Spirit from God or the spirit of the world from Satan and his fallen angels. You also know that you must be sealed with the Holy Spirit in order to be saved and gain entry into heaven. Humans get to exchange the spirit of the world for the Holy Spirit by putting their faith in Jesus Christ. The Nephilim were offspring of fallen angels and humans. They had the spirit of the world and could never exchange that spirit for the Spirit of God because they weren't human. They couldn't be redeemed by God. The pre-flood Nephilim died in the flood and became the evil spirits who roam the earth. For the same reason, God didn't offer redemption to the giants who lived after the flood, either.

Since God offers us a way to be saved and reconciled to him, I know it's hard to understand why it doesn't apply to angels or human-angel hybrids. Some things we just aren't meant to understand on this side of heaven. Jesus would have to be a human-angel hybrid and completely God in order to save hybrids. He'd have to be completely angel and yet God in order to save angels. He is neither of those. Jesus is completely human yet also completely God. That's why he was the perfect sacrifice for our sins. Know that God sent Jesus specifically for you. That's how special we are to him.

Do you see how Satan is assaulting the afterlife by making hybrids? He wants to keep people out of heaven and make sure they get sent to hell!

Fast forward to the present day. Satan is once again assaulting your afterlife by convincing you that you can become more than human. That you can be a hybrid human. And honestly, it's not a very hard sell. Have you noticed that most of the popular movies and TV shows these days seem to revolve around super humans? Consider Captain America, the Winter Soldier, the X-Men, Spider-Man, Thor, Aquaman, and Wonder Woman. The superheroes of comic books have never been more popular. So, if you were told that you could have eagle eyesight, see in the dark with cat eyes, breath underwater like a fish, have the strength of a grizzly bear, or shoot spider webs out of your arms with just a simple injection that would alter your DNA, would you want to do it? You know full well that a whole ton of people would want to do it. Maybe even you would. Well, the technology already exists. It has for a while. They're using CRISPR/CAS9.[2] Check out these headlines and see for yourself.

> "US Senate Passes Bill To Give Billions Of Dollars In Funding For Human-Animal Hybrid Experiments"[3]
> "Why Scientists Have Been Creating Chimeras In The Lab For Decades"[4]
> "Startups Are Helping Armies Create Legions Of Super-Soldiers"[5]
> "Researchers Inject Human DNA Into Monkeys, Recreating Pre-Flood Sin Of The 'Nephilim'"[6]
> "Japan Approves First Human-Animal Embryo Experiments"[7]
> "Scientists Successfully Made Sheep-Human Hybrids In 2018"[8]
> "Israeli Doctors Develop 'Pig-Human' Hybrid Organ For Transplant"[9]

Now, how about if you were told that you could be more than that even? That you could be half human and half horse, like a centaur? Satan's Hollywood propaganda machine is working hard in this space too. Consider the new popular TV show on Netflix, *Sweet Tooth*.[10] It's about human-animal hybrids that start being born after a virus has wiped out most of mankind. Or think of the popularity of mythology stories like Percy Jackson that depict not only human-animal hybrids but demigods who are the children of an immortal and a human. Yes, immortals. And this is where the genetic altering gets really tempting for mankind and brings us right back to Noah's day.

What do you think an angel looks like? We've discussed this a little bit in prior chapters. Do you think they look like the chubby little cherubs depicted in ancient art? Nope. The Bible reveals several kinds of angelic beings. They don't all look alike. Some look like people, like the angel Gabriel (Daniel 8:15-16). The seraphim have six wings (Isaiah 6:2). The four living beings that surround God's throne look human, except that they have four faces (human, lion, ox, eagle), wings, human hands, and feet like hooves (Ezekiel 1:5-10). Wow! That looks like something we'd call a hybrid, doesn't it? I wonder what the angels looked like that left heaven during Noah's day. Depictions of hybrid humans fill ancient literature and art. I don't think it's a coincidence. Satan is assaulting heaven and your afterlife with hybrids because he wants you to desire to be like an angel.

Perhaps you've heard of this popular show on the History Channel, *Ancient Aliens*.[11] It promotes the hypothesis that long ago, aliens not only seeded or created mankind, but also taught us engineering, science, technology, and other advanced skills. That sounds like a lie straight from the pit of hell, doesn't it? Satan is grooming people, brainwashing them really, with his alien deception. Consider most of those movies I mentioned earlier have an extraterrestrial component to them too. The Avengers fought bad guys from space and other planets. Just think of how influential *Star Wars*, *Star Trek*, *Stargate*, and *E.T.* have been on the last few generations.[12] People are absolutely obsessed with aliens! They're quick to believe that aliens exist all while dismissing that God does. Well, aliens do exist. They're fallen angels in disguise! I exposed this in my book *Rapture 911: What To Do If You're Left Behind*.[13] There's no question. If it acts and talks like a fallen angel, then it is. Other Bible prophecy authors are pulling the curtain back on this one too. Don't be fooled by Satan's deception here, it's imperative!

Let's say all of the Christians were gone, raptured, and a bunch of beings claiming to be from outer space or some distant galaxy arrived on the planet. We believers can't be here you see, we'd expose Satan's deception and ruin it for him. So, we have to be out of the way first. The beings might say they're advanced aliens or even say they're angels. If they had superpowers, didn't die when people tried to kill them, didn't get sick, didn't ever get weak, and didn't even need to sleep, then people would start to realize that they're immortal. People would consider them gods. People would want to be like them, wouldn't they? I'm sure some women would even want to marry them and have hybrid children. And if these beings told mankind that they certainly could be like them and that they too could live forever, would people believe them? And since we already have the technology to make hybrids, and Satan wants to deceive us, what do you think would happen? Lots of people would willingly become a human-alien hybrid or human-angel hybrid! You know they would.

Satan is assaulting the afterlife with hybridism because it's deceiving people about how to live forever, how to obtain salvation and be eligible for heaven, and it's attacking God's promises of what people will be in heaven.

So, this hybridism naturally brings up the question of how human do you have to be in order to be eligible for salvation? What if someone got eagle eye vision? Does that make them not human enough? You know, it doesn't take much genetic altering to make you not human. Chimpanzees are 98.8% genetically similar to humans.[14] That means they're only 1.2% genetically different than us. God said don't cross breed. It's a command. If you become a human-angel, it's a certainty that you can't be saved. Don't be tempted to alter your DNA by inserting non-human things into it. It's not worth risking your salvation. Don't let Satan steal the heavenly afterlife that God wants for you because you want to be more than you are right now.

This brings me to Satan's assault about being more than human. God doesn't want us to envy other creations. You know, when God created us and everything on the earth that we're the only thing that God called very good (Genesis 1). You are made in the very image of God (Genesis 1:27). You are special. You're going to have a glorified human body in the afterlife that won't break down and that will be able to do cool things like teleport, since Jesus's resurrected body did (John 20:19), and walk on water (Matthew 14:25-29). So, you don't need to try with all your might to achieve a super body today. It's one of God's promises that we're meant to look forward to, not try to achieve by our own means ahead of time.

The apostle Paul answered the question we all want to know. What kind of body are we going to have after we die?

> But someone will say, "How are the dead raised?" and, "With what kind of body do they come?" You foolish one, that which you yourself sow is not made alive unless it dies. That which you sow, you don't sow the body that will be, but a bare grain, maybe of wheat, or of some other kind. But God gives it a body even as it pleased him, and to each seed a body of its own. All flesh is not the same flesh, but there is one flesh of men, another flesh of animals, another of fish, and another of birds. There are also celestial bodies and terrestrial bodies; but the glory of the celestial differs from that of the terrestrial. ... So also is the resurrection of the dead. The body is sown perishable; it is raised imperishable. It is sown in dishonor; it is raised in glory. It is sown in weakness; it is raised in power. (1 Corinthians 15:35-40, 42-43)

He tells us that each seed has a "body of its own." Remember from Genesis 3:15 that both the woman and the devil have seed. They are two different kinds of seed. We're also told that flesh is different. Humans have one kind of flesh and other creations a different flesh. You were not seeded by ancient aliens or ancient angels. They have a different seed than you do. You aren't going to become a hybrid anything in the afterlife. You won't even become an entirely different creation in the afterlife. So, you won't become an animal or insect or plant after you die. And you most certainly will not turn into an angel in the afterlife! You were created by God and fashioned into his very image. That will not change.

Satan wants you to think that you'll become an angel in the afterlife because he wants your worship before you die. He wants you to desire that false afterlife so much today that you'd alter your DNA and become part angel just to get a taste of it. He knows if you do it that it'll be your demise. Do you want angel wings so bad in heaven because you want to experience the freedom of flying? That's not how Jesus gets around. Other than teleporting, he flies around on the backs of angels (Psalm 18:10, Ezekiel 1).

Yes, the angels are more powerful than us today. We were created lower than them (Hebrews 2:7). However, it's believers who will judge the angels (1 Corinthians 6:3) and rule the restored earth with Jesus during the millennial kingdom (Hebrews 1:13). Angels are servants of

God, created to care for us believers (Hebrews 1:14). You won't be lower than the angels for much longer.

By feeding our desire to be more than human, Satan is prepping mankind for his ultimate deception. It'll be the climax in his war on our afterlife. And it's going to answer the question I know you've got on your mind. How on earth would someone even be able to become a human-angel hybrid today? Cause it's not like angels are down here living among us out in the open. Well, that's going to change real soon. Let's see what's in store.

PART 5

SATAN'S ASSAULT REACHES A CLIMAX

CHAPTER 17 - A RETURN TO THE BEGINNING

Satan's assault on the afterlife reaches its climax after the rapture, during the tribulation period. During this period of time, Satan is going to unleash his full fury against God, God's dwelling place, and all those who dwell in heaven. It will be the apex of what we've been discussing throughout this book. In the Scripture below, "the beast" is the Antichrist and "the dragon" is Satan.

> The beast which I saw was like a leopard, and his feet were like those of a bear, and his mouth like the mouth of a lion. The dragon gave him his power, his throne, and great authority. ... A mouth speaking great things and blasphemy was given to him. Authority to make war for forty-two months was given to him. He opened his mouth for blasphemy against God, to blaspheme his name, his dwelling, and those who dwell in heaven. It was given to him to make war with the saints and to overcome them. Authority over every tribe, people, language, and nation was given to him. (Revelation 13:2, 5-7)

The Antichrist will have authority over everyone on the earth. Halfway through his seven-year reign, he'll be at war directly against God's holy people, "the saints," for 42 months. Satan's tactics during this great battle will not be new, however. Satan was so successful in assaulting the afterlife in the garden of Eden that he's going to return to the exact same strategy he used before. Satan is going to return to what he did in the beginning, in his first attack. Let's revisit what happened back then.

> Now the serpent was more subtle than any animal of the field which Yahweh God had made. He said to the woman, "Has God really said, 'You shall not eat of any tree of the garden'?" The woman said to the serpent, "We may eat fruit from the trees of the garden, but not the fruit of the tree which is in the middle of the garden. God has said, 'You shall not eat of it. You shall not touch it, lest you die.'" The serpent said to the woman, "You won't really die, for God knows that in the day you eat it, your eyes will be opened, and you will be like God, knowing good and evil." When the woman saw that the tree was good for food, and that it was a delight to

the eyes, and that the tree was to be desired to make one wise, she took some of its fruit, and ate. Then she gave some to her husband with her, and he ate it, too. (Genesis 3:1-6)

Remember that "the serpent" is Satan, "the woman" is Eve, and "her husband" is Adam. First, Eve listened to Satan, a fallen angel in disguise. Then, Satan convinced her to question God's truthfulness by asking her "has God really said?" Then, he convinced Eve that God lied to her and that she wouldn't die if she ate the forbidden fruit. Instead, she'd be like God. Which she obviously desired. So, she willingly ate the fruit and so did Adam. The result of Adam and Eve's disobedience to God was their banishment from the garden of Eden, their eventual death, the invasion of sin into the world, and the curse on all mankind and the earth.

Satan's going to follow this exact same pattern during the tribulation period. First, he's going to convince mankind to listen to him, a fallen angel, again. How is he going to do this? Well, we know the Antichrist reigns over the entire earth and that he's possessed by Satan. The Antichrist is Satan in disguise, just like the serpent in the garden of Eden. He's going to be in power shortly after the rapture (which we'll discuss in Chapter 19). It'll be a time of chaos the world has never known before. Since the Antichrist reigns over the whole earth, clearly all the people listen to him. He'll have answers and will be able to bring peace that the world will be desperate for. In fact, they're going to do more than listen to him, they're going to worship him. "They" are all the people on the earth.

> They worshiped the dragon because he gave his authority to the beast; and they worshiped the beast, saying, "Who is like the beast? Who is able to make war with him?" ... All who dwell on the earth will worship him, everyone whose name has not been written from the foundation of the world in the book of life of the Lamb who has been killed. (Revelation 13:4, 8)

Satan is assaulting the afterlife through the Antichrist's reign. It's an assault against Jesus, the rightful ruler of the planet. You see, Jesus is coming again to reign on the earth and receive all the worship and glory that's due him. Satan wants to prevent that. He wants to rule instead. He wants all the glory and worship for himself.

There are many reasons why people will worship the Antichrist. The biggest reason is that he's going to pretend that he's God (2 Thessalonians 2:3-4, Daniel 11:36-37). It fits. Satan wants to be God. So, he's going to lie and say that he is. The Antichrist is going to reign during a very perilous time on the planet. There will be widespread famine and disasters of biblical proportions. I'm sure he's going to offer people food, health, and safety in exchange for worshiping him. That's what his mark is all about (which we're going to get to in a minute). Also, since the Antichrist is possessed by Satan, he's going to be able to perform signs and wonders. But they'll be illusions, fake.

> He whose coming is according to the working of Satan with all power and signs and lying wonders, and with all deception of wickedness. (2 Thessalonians 2:9-10)

In fact, one of the Antichrist's signs is going to be his own fake resurrection after he fakes being fatally wounded (Revelation 13:3). Do you see how Satan is going to assault the afterlife here? Not only is he directly attacking God and his authority, but he's also mocking God's power over death.

When the Antichrist declares himself God, he's going to do it in the Third Temple that the Jewish people build in Jerusalem. We discussed this in Chapter 3.1. Then he's going to pollute the temple with something sacrilegious. This is yet another assault by Satan on the afterlife because we know the temple is modeled after the one in heaven (Hebrews 8:1-5).

Second, Satan is going to get mankind to question God's truthfulness. This will be easy because there will be a shortage of biblical truth being taught and preached. You see, all the believers will be raptured and taken up into the present heaven by Jesus prior to the Antichrist's reign on earth (John 14:1-3, 2 Thessalonians 2:1-8). So, there won't be any Christians who know the real God and God's Word to combat the onslaught of lies that will be coming from the Antichrist.

Remember that the Antichrist's specialty is blasphemy. People are going to believe what he'll say against Jesus and the lies he'll tell about what happened to everyone who was raptured. He's going to discredit the Bible and say the God of the Bible isn't real. Yes, there will be the two witnesses preaching God's truth and salvation in Jerusalem for 42 months before the Antichrist declares himself God. However, we know that most people won't listen to them because the people celebrate when the Antichrist murders both of them (Revelation 11:1-12). Also remember that the Antichrist will already have convinced everyone to worship him. So, the people are going to easily believe the lies that he tells.

Now, the last three tactics used by Satan in the garden of Eden all go together. Satan needs to convince mankind that man won't die, that man can be like God, and to eat the forbidden fruit in order to achieve those things. All of these revolve around the mark of the beast. Let's take a look at what God tells us about this.

In this Scripture, "he causes" is referring to the False Prophet. He'll be the right-hand man of the Antichrist and force everyone to get a mark.

> He causes all, the small and the great, the rich and the poor, and the free and the slave, to be given marks on their right hands or on their foreheads; and that no one would be able to buy or to sell unless he has that mark, which is the name of the beast or the number of his name. (Revelation 13:16-17)

Now, we're told this mark enables people to buy and sell. However, I don't believe it's going to be a simple barcode or chip. These two Scriptures reveal why.

> Another angel, a third, followed them, saying with a great voice, "If anyone worships the beast and his image, and receives a mark on his forehead or on his hand, he also will drink of the wine of the wrath of God, which is prepared unmixed in the cup of his anger. He will be tormented with fire and sulfur in the presence of the holy angels and in the presence of the Lamb." (Revelation 14:9-10)

> "But when the Son of Man comes in his glory, and all the holy angels with him, then he will sit on the throne of his glory. Before him all the nations will be gathered, and he will separate them one from another, as a shepherd separates the sheep from the goats. He will set the sheep on his right hand, but the goats on the left. Then the King will tell those on his

right hand, 'Come, blessed of my Father, inherit the Kingdom prepared for you from the foundation of the world'; ... Then he will say also to those on the left hand, 'Depart from me, you cursed, into the eternal fire which is prepared for the devil and his angels.' " (Matthew 25:31-34, 41)

In the first Scripture, God is literally going to send an angel down from heaven to fly around the planet and warn people against getting the mark. This reveals the seriousness of the situation. God wants everyone to be informed. No one will have an excuse when they get the mark.

The second Scripture is a truth that Jesus revealed during his first coming. He tells us what he's going to do at his second coming, which happens right after the tribulation period. Jesus often referred to himself as the "Son of Man." Looking at both Scriptures together we realize the punishment for getting the mark is being thrown into the lake of fire. That's the eternal hell. Anyone who gets the mark completely skips the present hell and the white throne judgment and instead goes straight to the eternal hell. Yikes! Why is that? There must be something about the mark that's as offensive to God as you can get. Something that Jesus's death on the cross cannot absolve.

The Bible doesn't specifically tell us what the mark is or does, but I believe we can easily infer it. I believe the mark is Satan's genetic weapon. His ultimate assault on the afterlife. Because the mark will contain angel DNA. I think it'll turn people into human-angel hybrids and make it impossible for them to exchange their spirit of the world for the Holy Spirit. Just like what happened before the flood. This is Satan's assault that I warned you about in the prior chapter!

It perfectly fits Satan's tactic against Eve. Satan will convince mankind that they don't have to die. That they can become immortal and have special powers, like the angels and like the Antichrist who they'll worship like God in the flesh. All they need to do is get this little mark. Get some angel DNA injected into themselves via a microneedle patch that they can apply on their hand or forehead. Nobody wants to die. Everyone wants to live forever.

You know those microneedle patches are already being used. Scientists are even exploring the possibility of using them to deliver childhood immunizations. They could even contain quantum dots, nanoparticles that reflect light and glow under infrared light, that make it easy to detect someone immunized.[1] What's more is that scientists are now successfully storing information into DNA.[2] That's right, your own DNA could one day store all your banking information or medical history. Combine all of that technology together and you have the tool that might be used to deliver the mark of the beast. A little microneedle patch that delivers human DNA altering angel genes along with information that enables someone to buy and sell.

Can't you envision it happening? Let's say you saw the most magnificent looking angel God created. That's Satan by the way. And he displayed awesome power, lied and told you that he was God the Father, and then he told you how to live forever. That you just need to apply this little patch and become like him. Would you believe him? How would you know that he's really Satan and not God?

We believers would know because the Bible tells us to ask him about Jesus. Satan and the Antichrist are going to tell every lie they can think of about Jesus. To them Jesus is Satan. But people who don't know the Bible and who never believed what Christians told them about Jesus are ripe for being deceived by Satan's lies. They are going to line up to get his mark. The masses will no doubt eat this modern-day forbidden fruit. And just like Eve, the people won't realize that they're being deceived. This is why it's so imperative that you share the gospel with those you care about before it's too late.

And eating this new forbidden fruit is going to have the same consequence that it did in the past. I'm not talking about the consequence that the fruit on the Tree of the Knowledge of Good and Evil had for Adam and Eve, and all of us for that matter. I'm referring to the sin of being more than human, of being a human-angel hybrid. It's what we discussed in the prior chapter. That's why everyone who gets the mark, who I believe will be a hybrid, will be thrown into the eternal hell. Satan will achieve a small victory in his assault on the afterlife through the death and demise of countless humans who believe his lie about living forever.

I believe this is why when Jesus returns at his second coming the Antichrist and the False Prophet both get sent immediately to the lake of fire. Remember, "the beast" is the Antichrist.

> The beast was taken, and with him the false prophet who worked the signs in his sight, with which he deceived those who had received the mark of

> the beast and those who worshiped his image. These two were thrown alive into the lake of fire that burns with sulfur. (Revelation 19:20)

If they were human, I believe Jesus would just kill them and they'd go to the present hell to await the great white throne judgment. Yet, Jesus doesn't even kill them first which is a bit curious, don't you think? Instead, they get sent to the eternal hell immediately. How can they live in the eternal hell without an immortal body? You think it's because they already had one? God created the eternal hell for the fallen angels (Matthew 25:41). Maybe you think it's because they'll both be possessed by Satan and that's why they get thrown into the lake of fire. Well, that's not what happened to Judas, the disciple who betrayed Jesus. He was possessed by Satan too (John 13:26-27), but he died (Acts 1:16-19). I'm convinced it's because the Antichrist and the False Prophet will be human-angel hybrids who genetically modify themselves to be more than human.

Perhaps you think this is out of the universe crazy. You wonder where is all this angel DNA going to come from anyway? That people wouldn't believe this is possible unless they saw an angel firsthand. Well, it's coming! During the tribulation period people are going to be absolutely aware that God, heaven, and the angels exist. At some point during the tribulation period, God is going to roll back the sky and reveal heaven.

> The sky was removed like a scroll when it is rolled up. ... The kings of the earth, the princes, the commanding officers, the rich, the strong, and every slave and free person, hid themselves in the caves and in the rocks of the mountains. They told the mountains and the rocks, "Fall on us, and hide us from the face of him who sits on the throne, and from the wrath of the Lamb." (Revelation 6:14-16)

Everyone is going to see God's throne room. The "Lamb" is Jesus. He's surrounded by millions of holy angels (Revelation 5:11). You know, you'd think this would freak people out and cause them to adjust their beliefs. Perhaps reconsider things they heard from the Antichrist in a new light per se. You'd think they'd repent and turn to Jesus for salvation. But they don't. In fact, the people essentially shake their fists at Jesus in defiance (Revelation 9:20). They also refuse to repent of their "sorceries" (Revelation 9:21). That word could refer to drugs or witchcraft. I think genetic manipulation that turns someone into a hybrid could certainly be considered a type of witchcraft. People won't repent about getting the mark. That's because they want to be more than human.

Satan's assault on the afterlife will take an ominous turn when the sky rolls back. He will have convinced the people to directly assault God, heaven, and those who dwell there all by themselves, no deception even needed. Why would the people do this? Perhaps they don't believe that they're seeing God in the sky? Instead, they've fully bought into Satan's lie that he's God. It could go back to the mark. Perhaps it renders them incapable of recognizing God's authority and worshiping him. Sounds like the spirit of the fallen angels, doesn't it?

In addition to the window of heaven, there will be three holy angels flying around the whole earth, halfway during the tribulation period (Revelation 14:6-13). One will preach the gospel, one will warn against getting the mark, and another will proclaim the fall of Babylon. Everyone will see them.

And there's more. There will be hordes of wicked fallen angels patrolling the earth and inflicting horrors upon mankind because God sends a holy angel to unlock the bottomless pit where some evil angels and demonic creatures live, and to release four evil angels who've been bound at the Euphrates River (Revelation 9). What used to live in heaven will literally assault the earth and mankind because they want to destroy our afterlife.

As a quick aside, you need to know that God's judgments during the tribulation period, like allowing the fallen angels to wreak havoc, have a purpose. He's afflicting the fallen angels (Isaiah 24:21-23) and people who didn't put their faith in Jesus before the rapture. God's demonstration of awesome power during this period is meant to reveal God, expose the false power of the Antichrist, and ultimately get people to repent and turn to Jesus for salvation (Jeremiah 36:1-3, Revelation 9:20). This has always been one of the reasons God allows hard or bad things to happen to people. It's to get us to come to him and rely on him for help, for salvation, and to grow our faith (1 Peter 1:6-12). Unfortunately, most people won't see it this way because during this time, God will also be giving people who don't want anything to do with him exactly what they want. They'll have Satan as their ruler, an anything goes sinful culture, and no Christians. To people opposed to God, it'll be heaven on earth.

As if all those angels being visible wasn't enough, Satan is also going to reveal himself.

> They worshiped the dragon because he gave his authority to the beast. (Revelation 13:4)

The people "worshiped the dragon." There's no way Satan is going to stay hidden in the heavenly dimension and let the Antichrist and False Prophet take all the glory. He's going to make his presence known. You know what else, I don't think he'll have a choice. Even though Satan and the fallen angels got kicked out of residing in heaven because they sinned and started this war, they still have access to God in his throne room (Luke 10:18, Job 1:6-7). They dwell on the earth, but still operate in the heavenly dimension that we aren't able to see. Well, during the tribulation period, they get kicked out permanently and lose all of their heavenly privileges.

> "The time for judging this world has come, when Satan, the ruler of this world, will be cast out." (John 12:31 NLT)

> There was war in the sky. Michael and his angels made war on the dragon. The dragon and his angels made war. They didn't prevail. No place was found for them any more in heaven. The great dragon was thrown down, the old serpent, he who is called the devil and Satan, the deceiver of the whole world. He was thrown down to the earth, and his angels were thrown down with him. I heard a loud voice in heaven, saying, "Now the salvation, the power, and the Kingdom of our God, and the authority of his Christ has come; for the accuser of our brothers has been thrown down, who accuses them before our God day and night. They overcame him because of the Lamb's blood, and because of the word of their testimony. They didn't love their life, even to death. Therefore rejoice, heavens, and you who dwell in them. Woe to the earth and to the sea, because the devil has gone down to you, having great wrath, knowing that he has but a short time." (Revelation 12:7-12)

"No place was found for them any more in heaven." I think this means that the fallen angels can't even access the heavenly dimension anymore. They'll be on the earth and visible to humans. We know this event hasn't happened yet because it speaks about the "Kingdom of God" and the "authority of Christ" having come. Jesus will setup his kingdom at the end of the tribulation period. The fallen angels get banished before that, sometime shortly after the rapture. It also references the tribulation saints, "they didn't love their life, even to death." Those are the people who refuse the mark, who put their faith in Jesus instead. So, this event must happen during the tribulation period. And just like that, Satan's garden of Eden tactics get him the fate that God leveled on Adam and Eve for their sin - banishment from heaven. Satan will be relegated to earth and earth alone. Everyone on earth will see him. And not only him, but all of his fallen angels will also be with him.

So, there you have it. That's how mankind is going to buy into becoming a human-angel hybrid. Fallen angels are going to be everywhere. But the vast majority of people aren't going to realize they're fallen. The level of deception during this time is going to be almost incomprehensible. God warned us that this strong delusion is coming (2 Thessalonians 2:9-11).

God also warned us that this genetic mixing won't work. God gave the prophet Daniel visions of all the world kingdoms that would succeed Babylon and King Nebuchadnezzar up until Jesus's millennial kingdom. He had a vision of four beasts, of which the last beast had ten horns. Three of the horns were plucked out by a fourth horn that arose speaking blasphemous words (Daniel 7:7-8). The horns represent rulers. The last horn represents the Antichrist.

Daniel also had a vision of a giant statue of which the ten toes depict the last kingdom (Daniel 2:40-43). The toes represent rulers. Daniel's visions are further clarified by John's revelation that the last beast is a large red dragon with seven heads and ten horns. His name is Satan (Revelation 12:3-4). So now that you understand that the last kingdom is Satan's kingdom, with the Antichrist ruling, I want to reveal what Daniel was told about the ten toes.

> As the toes of the feet were part of iron, and part of clay, so the kingdom will be partly strong and partly brittle. Whereas you saw the iron mixed with miry clay, they will mingle themselves with the seed of men; but they

won't cling to one another, even as iron does not mix with clay. (Daniel 2:42-43)

The toes are iron mixed with clay. What's curious here is that it says, "they will mingle themselves with the seed of men." The Bible does not tell us who the "they" is. Then it says, "they won't cling to one another." So, whatever this mixing is, it doesn't work. Well, since we know that these ten toes represent Satan's last kingdom and one of those toes is the Antichrist, what do you think the "they" refers to? I think it's fallen angels. And here God is warning us that mixing our human seed with their fallen angel seed won't work. Whatever Satan and the Antichrist promise during the tribulation period regarding the mark, like it'll turn you into an angel who can live forever, it won't work. I think it also reveals Satan's true nature. He's completely repelled by us humans. He doesn't desire to live with us, or mix with us per se. His intent is to destroy us.

Now, you've seen that during the tribulation period, Satan will assault the afterlife by convincing most of mankind to fall for the same type of deception that Adam and Eve did. He'll return to what worked for him at the very beginning of our creation. But he doesn't stop there. He knows that Jesus is coming back to earth at the end of the tribulation period. So, Satan will gather a huge army to war against Jesus upon his return. He'll return to the beginning once again. His very first assault was against God. He thought he could be like God. He still thinks he can beat God. This will be his last chance to stop our afterlife, to stop heaven from coming to earth.

In these verses, the one "called Faithful and True" is Jesus. The "armies which are in heaven" are believers who are in the present heaven, including anyone who gets raptured before the tribulation, and anyone who comes to faith in Jesus after the rapture and dies during the tribulation. The holy angels return with Jesus too (2 Thessalonians 1:7-8). The "beast," as you know, is the Antichrist.

> I saw the heaven opened, and behold, a white horse, and he who sat on it is called Faithful and True. In righteousness he judges and makes war. ... The armies which are in heaven, clothed in white, pure, fine linen, followed him on white horses. ... I saw the beast, the kings of the earth, and their armies, gathered together to make war against him who sat on

the horse and against his army. The beast was taken, and with him the false prophet who worked the signs in his sight, with which he deceived those who had received the mark of the beast and those who worshiped his image. These two were thrown alive into the lake of fire that burns with sulfur. ... I saw an angel coming down out of heaven, having the key of the abyss and a great chain in his hand. He seized the dragon, the old serpent, who is the devil and Satan, who deceives the whole inhabited earth, and bound him for a thousand years, and cast him into the abyss, and shut it and sealed it over him, that he should deceive the nations no more until the thousand years were finished. After this, he must be freed for a short time. (Revelation 19:11, 14, 19-20, 20:1-3)

In this epic culmination to the tribulation period, Satan takes one more stand against all of heaven—Jesus, believers, holy angels, and God's dwelling place, which has become earth. As you can see, Satan doesn't win. In fact, he's quickly defeated. It only takes one holy angel to send him to his temporary demise, "the abyss." Try as he might to assault the afterlife, our afterlife, Satan is doomed to fail.

But the war isn't over yet. God gives Satan one more final fight. Let's see how this war finally ends.

CHAPTER 18 - THE AFTERLIFE IS REJECTED

We've come to the last great battle in Satan's assault on the afterlife. At the end of Jesus's millennial reign, God lets Satan out of the bottomless pit.

> And after the thousand years, Satan will be released from his prison and he will come out to deceive the nations which are in the four corners of the earth, Gog and Magog, to gather them together to the war, whose number is as the sand of the sea. They went up over the width of the earth and surrounded the camp of the saints and the beloved city. Fire came down out of heaven from God and devoured them. The devil who deceived them was thrown into the lake of fire and sulfur, where the beast and the false prophet are also. They will be tormented day and night forever and ever. (Revelation 20:7-10)

Satan goes against "the camp of the saints and the beloved city." That's Jerusalem. That's where Jesus Christ has setup his throne on the earth (Zechariah 8:2-3, 9:9-10, 14:16). Satan will rise up against Jesus and essentially challenge his rulership of the planet, which Jesus has made heaven on earth. Satan wants to rule heaven and earth. That's been his desire from the beginning.

Now, Satan isn't just attacking Jesus and those who live in Jerusalem. Notice it says his army went over "the width of the earth." The word that's used in the original Greek language, *platos*, is used four times in the Bible. Each time it denotes great breadth, something almost incomprehensible in size (Ephesians 3:18, Revelation 21:16). It seems to me that Satan will be assaulting the entire planet. I think that's because believers will be living everywhere, not just in Jerusalem. And the reason he assaults believers is because believers contain the Holy Spirit. The very Spirit of God. Believers are essentially dwelling places for God, temples (1 Corinthians 3:16-17). And you learned in this book that Satan desecrates holy temples (Ezekiel 28:18). In fact, that's another reason why Satan is going to go against Jerusalem. The Millennial Temple is going to be there in all its wonderful glory (Ezekiel 40-43).

In Satan's epic last stand against all of heaven, there isn't even a battle! God shoots fire down from heaven and destroys the entire army. Then Satan is thrown into the eternal hell, "the lake of fire." That's it, game over. It's a bit shocking to me that it ends so quickly and in a way that seems so effortless. We tend to make Satan bigger than he is, don't we? We must remember that he's just an angel. A being that God created. God is infinitely bigger than our enemy.

However, I think what's most shocking about this last stand is the size of Satan's army. He's able to gather people from all over the earth. The number of people, "as the sand of the sea," means they can't even be counted. Now, Jesus's millennial kingdom starts out with only believers. The people who survived the tribulation period and put their faith in Jesus and the immortal heaven dwellers who return with him. But, a thousand years later, there will be generations of people who choose not to believe everything Jesus did in the past. People who don't like how Jesus rules. There will be people who reject our afterlife, Jesus's heaven on earth. I'm referring only to non-immortals here. The immortal heaven dwellers, which you could be one of, cannot reject the afterlife because their eternal destination is already sealed and guaranteed. In this Scripture, "Yahweh" is God.

> But they refused to listen, and turned their backs, and stopped their ears, that they might not hear. Yes, they made their hearts as hard as flint, lest they might hear the law and the words which Yahweh of Armies had sent by his Spirit by the former prophets. Therefore great wrath came from Yahweh of Armies. (Zechariah 7:11-12)

We see that some people will refuse to listen. They won't read the Bible or any other account that believers will write during the millennial period. If you've put your faith in Jesus and are among the immortals ruling with Jesus, they aren't going to believe your testimony, either. I'm sure there's even going to be video footage, movies, and documentaries of the Antichrist's reign during the tribulation period and Jesus's second coming. That won't matter. In the verses below, the nations who were left that came against Jerusalem is a reference to the people who survive the tribulation period and put their faith in Jesus. The "King" is Jesus.

> It will happen that everyone who is left of all the nations that came against

> Jerusalem will go up from year to year to worship the King, Yahweh of Armies, and to keep the feast of booths. It will be that whoever of all the families of the earth doesn't go up to Jerusalem to worship the King, Yahweh of Armies, on them there will be no rain. If the family of Egypt doesn't go up and doesn't come, neither will it rain on them. This will be the plague with which Yahweh will strike the nations that don't go up to keep the feast of booths. (Zechariah 14:16-18)

So, everyone who makes it into the millennial period will be expected to go to Jerusalem once a year to worship King Jesus. We learn that some people will refuse to make the trip because there's a consequence for not going—no rain. We don't know how long it'll take for people and generations to start rejecting the afterlife, but they will. It reminds me of a quote from the movie, *The Matrix*. Agent Smith told Morpheus: "Did you know that the first Matrix was designed to be a perfect human world where none suffered, where everyone would be happy? It was a disaster. No one would accept the program."[1]

So, what do they choose instead? This Scripture is a description of life in the millennial period. The "God of Jacob" is Jesus. He's going to be the one ruling over the world from Jerusalem (Zion) and teaching people his ways.

> But in the latter days, it will happen that the mountain of Yahweh's temple will be established on the top of the mountains, and it will be exalted above the hills; and peoples will stream to it. Many nations will go and say, "Come! Let's go up to the mountain of Yahweh, and to the house of the God of Jacob; and he will teach us of his ways, and we will walk in his paths." For the law will go out of Zion, and Yahweh's word from Jerusalem; and he will judge between many peoples, and will decide concerning strong nations afar off. They will beat their swords into plowshares, and their spears into pruning hooks. Nation will not lift up sword against nation, neither will they learn war any more. But every man will sit under his vine and under his fig tree. No one will make them afraid, for the mouth of Yahweh of Armies has spoken. Indeed all the nations may walk in the name of their gods, but we will walk in the name of Yahweh our God forever and ever. (Micah 4:1-5)

Some people will "walk in the name of their gods." They won't want to see Jesus and hear his ways. It makes me really sad to see that some people will worship someone or something other than Jesus. A false god. And these people will do this without Satan's influence in the world (Revelation 20:3)! Sure, Satan comes back at the end and deceives people again. But it seems like the people he gathers will have already hardened their hearts against Jesus.

Throughout this book, we've discussed several ways in which Satan is assaulting our afterlife. Deceiving us with his lies just like he did to Eve and Adam. But it makes me wonder what would have happened if Satan hadn't tempted and deceived Eve. Would she and Adam have eventually rejected the perfect garden of Eden anyway all on their own? I think the answer is undoubtedly yes. Adam and Eve only had one rule to follow. I don't think it would have mattered what rule they were given, either. Eventually, someone would have broken it. Curiosity, to test God, to spite God, because they forgot the rule, because they took God's promises for granted, they decided they didn't need God anymore, etc. We're sinners by nature. That's why God had a plan to save us from the very beginning of creation (Ephesians 1:4-5). It doesn't matter if we're living in heaven on earth. We'll eventually reject that heaven because we'll believe a lie of our own making. It's the same lie that Satan believes. That he can be like God.

We must each come to realize that we cannot be like God. Instead, we can become children of God and heirs of all that is his. His glory, kingdom, and creation. We're sinners in need of a savior. I hope that you haven't rejected the afterlife that Jesus desires for you. He loves you and wants you to live with him in heaven. Right now, he's in the present heaven above, but he's coming back to earth very soon to setup heaven down here. You can be with Jesus when he returns! Trust me, you aren't going to reject the afterlife once you place your faith in Jesus. You'll be looking forward to it instead! That's because God designed it specifically for us and placed a longing for it in our hearts (Ecclesiastes 3:11). Join me in the next chapter where we'll discuss the rapture. You know, there's a reason Satan mocks it. You guessed it; he's assaulting the afterlife!

PART 6

SATAN ALREADY LOST HIS WAR

CHAPTER 19 - THE KING IS COMING

In the prior two chapters, you saw that Satan's assault comes to an end. That's the great news, Satan isn't going to win. He's already lost his assault on the afterlife. While he continues to win little victories, his defeat is guaranteed. In fact, he's been defeated by God throughout time, again and again.

When Satan first rebelled against heaven, God kicked him out of heaven in triumph (Luke 10:18). After Satan caused Adam and Eve to sin in the garden of Eden, God kicked him out of heaven on earth and then foretold his ultimate demise (Genesis 3:14-15).

Satan thought he had thwarted God's plan and was on his way to victory when he corrupted most of mankind with his wickedness and gene modification scheme. Yet, God defeated Satan with the flood and bound the other angels who sinned (Genesis 7:23, Jude 1:6).

Satan believed that he almost had the victory prior to the flood, so his gene pollution resumed. The giants returned and took up residence in God's promised land. Satan once again thought he had a victory over heaven because he successfully invaded the future land where God would establish his throne on earth. The Israelites were so scared of the giants that they refused to dwell there. But God defeated most of those giants while the Israelites wandered in the wilderness and then he sent the Israelites into the promised land to finish them off (Genesis 14, Exodus 33:1-3). Satan's weapon against heaven was destroyed.

And then I believe that Satan thought God had absolutely lost his mind when Jesus, God in the flesh, came down from heaven and lived among us. God in a human body. Satan believed it was God's fatal error. Satan knew he had the victory when he ensured Jesus was crucified (John 19). You see, Satan killed God. He'd finally defeated heaven. But Satan failed to realize that God has the power over life and death. That God controls the afterlife, not Satan. When Jesus rose from the grave, Satan lost his war against heaven (Revelation 1:18, Hebrews 2:14). That's when Jesus conquered sin and death and paved the way for all of us to be saved and inherit the heaven that Satan so desires. You defeated Satan's assault on your afterlife as soon as you placed your faith in Jesus (1 John 5:1-5).

But Satan's war isn't over yet. He still thinks he can win! He's going to continue to assault the afterlife in all the ways we've discussed in this book, right up until his final demise. He hates humanity with every molecule of his being and wants all of us to end up in hell. Well, God's going to give Satan another huge blow of defeat sometime very soon when he removes all of the living believers from the planet and takes them up into heaven (1 Corinthians 15:52-56). We're going to talk about the rapture a lot more in this chapter so that you can have even more confidence in God's victory. You see, Satan gets permanently kicked out of heaven at the rapture and it sends him into an absolute rage (Revelation 12:7-9).

While the tribulation period is going to be a living hell for the people who are left behind, many tribulation saints will defeat Satan's assault on their afterlife during that time (Revelation 12:11). You know that Satan loses his battle against all of heaven at the end of the tribulation period, at Jesus's second coming (Revelation 20:1-3). He's confined in prison for a thousand years before he's let out and marches his vast army against heaven once again. But the final epic battle never even begins. God rains fire on the army and throws Satan into hell (Revelation 20:7-10). You see, it's because Satan has already lost his assault on the afterlife. Heaven already has the victory!

You can rest assured that you have the victory too! You don't need to fear the climax of Satan's war when all the fallen angels are wreaking havoc on the planet. If you've put your faith in Jesus, you're going to get raptured before then.

I'm sure you've heard of the rapture. The word *rapture* means to be caught up, snatched away, seized, or carried off to another place of existence. It's Jesus's promise to remove all people who've put their faith in him from the planet before the Antichrist's reign and all the horrible judgments of the tribulation period. You can read a lot more about the rapture in my book *Rapture 911: What To Do If You're Left Behind*.[1] We're just going to go over the highlights here.

You see, contrary to what Satan will tell you, believers are not the intended target of God's wrath (1 Thessalonians 1:10, 5:9-10). You don't need to survive through the tribulation to prove yourself worthy of heaven. You can't earn your way into heaven. It's a gift. So, the removed believers will be residing safely in the present heaven. Think of it this way. As a believer, you're an ambassador of heaven (Ephesians 6:20). When war here on earth breaks out between nations, ambassadors get recalled back to their home country. That's what God is doing in the rapture, calling all ambassadors home. This also means it's an event that happens separate from and prior to Jesus's second coming.

Satan wants to do everything he possibly can to keep you out of heaven. He wants you to suffer in the tribulation period, worship him, and then die the second death. This is one reason Satan assaults the rapture. Now, Satan will lie and tell you that the word *rapture* isn't even in the Bible. He also lies and says Jesus didn't teach it and neither did any of the ancient church, his disciples. Well, let's see the truth for ourselves.

Jesus most certainly taught about the rapture! Multiple times he told his followers to be watching for his return. He even told us what to be watching for. In this Scripture below, Jesus is the one speaking. He's talking to his disciples.

> "Don't let your heart be troubled. Believe in God. Believe also in me. In my Father's house are many homes. If it weren't so, I would have told you. I am going to prepare a place for you. If I go and prepare a place for you, I will come again, and will receive you to myself; that where I am, you may be there also." (John 14:1-3)

Jesus told his disciples to believe in God and in "me" which is himself. Then he says there are "many homes" in his "father's house." That's God's house. He was leaving to go "prepare a place" for them there. We know that God's house is in the present heaven. So Jesus was leaving for the present heaven, and he would come get them at a later time. This was the next thing Jesus wanted them to be expecting: his future return to get them. The phrase "receive you to myself" means to take to one's own self. That's literally what happens in the rapture. Jesus will take the believers to himself. He will do this so that believers can be where he is. Jesus is currently in the present heaven. In the rapture, Jesus will meet the believers in the clouds and take them to himself in heaven. This Scripture applies to anyone who puts their faith in Jesus. If you put your faith in Jesus, you get this promise too. Jesus has a place prepared just for you too in the present heaven.

Since Satan doesn't want you to have any part of this promise, he assaults the rapture by confusing it with Jesus's second coming. That's when Jesus physically appears on the planet again. But this doesn't make any sense. The two events are distinctly different. At Jesus's second coming, believers will already be with him in the present heaven and will be coming with him to earth. Jesus won't be receiving or taking anyone to himself at his second coming. Also remember that once Jesus returns to earth physically at the second coming that he sets up his millennial kingdom and after that creates a new earth. He doesn't ever leave and go back to heaven. That's because heaven will have essentially moved to earth. So, Jesus is clearly talking about the rapture, not his second coming.

The apostle Paul wrote this Scripture. He saw the resurrected Jesus face-to-face. He wrote about the rapture a lot. Don't believe Satan's lie that this is a new modern-day concept.

> But we don't want you to be ignorant, brothers, concerning those who have fallen asleep, so that you don't grieve like the rest, who have no hope. For if we believe that Jesus died and rose again, even so God will bring with him those who have fallen asleep in Jesus. For this we tell you by the word of the Lord, that we who are alive, who are left until the coming of the Lord, will in no way precede those who have fallen asleep. For the Lord himself will descend from heaven with a shout, with the voice of the archangel and with God's trumpet. The dead in Christ will rise first, then we who are alive, who are left, will be caught up together with them in the clouds, to meet the Lord in the air. So we will be with the Lord forever. Therefore comfort one another with these words. (1 Thessalonians 4:13-18)

Notice the phrase "caught up." In Latin it's translated *rapio*. It's where we get the English word *rapture* from. This Scripture tells us about the rapture. Jesus will come down from heaven and gather believers in the clouds with him. It tells us why Jesus takes them; it's because they believed Jesus died and rose again. The people who will be taken are described as "alive" and "who are left until the coming of the Lord." They aren't going to be the only ones Jesus takes. We also learn that "the dead in Christ" will be gathered too. These are people who had put their faith in Jesus, but already died. Death is also referenced in the Scripture as "fallen asleep." They died between the resurrection of Jesus and the rapture. Yes, they're already with Jesus in the present heaven; however, this is when they get their new body, which you'll see clearly in a bit. This Scripture also gives us a glimpse of what everyone gathered will be doing. It says they "will be with the Lord forever." That means from this event forward they'll be with Jesus, the Lord, for all eternity.

Here's another description of the rapture from Paul the apostle.

> Now I say this, brothers, that flesh and blood can't inherit God's Kingdom; neither does the perishable inherit imperishable. Behold, I tell you a mystery. We will not all sleep, but we will all be changed, in a moment, in the twinkling of an eye, at the last trumpet. For the trumpet will sound and the dead will be raised incorruptible, and we will be changed. For this perishable body must become imperishable, and this mortal must put on immortality. But when this perishable body will have become imperishable, and this mortal will have put on immortality, then what is written will happen: "Death is swallowed up in victory." (1 Corinthians 15:50-54)

"Flesh and blood" is a reference to our current bodies. They're temporary and not eternal. That's why they can't live in God's kingdom, which is heaven. Paul tells us not everyone will "sleep" which means some people won't die. Instead, those people who won't die will be changed in a moment. This will happen at the sound of a trumpet. That trumpet was mentioned in the prior Scripture we looked at too. We learn some extra details about what happens to the people Jesus gathers. They get new immortal bodies that are suitable for living in heaven for eternity. In that moment, a perishable body that could die will be transformed into an imperishable and immortal body. This new body applies to believers in heaven as well. The "dead in Christ" from the prior Scripture are described in these verses as "the dead will be raised incorruptible." Don't worry, the Old Testament believers who are in the present heaven get a new body too, just not until the second coming (Daniel 12:1-3, 13).

Another reason the rapture isn't a new concept is because the Old Testament speaks of it as well. I think the best depiction of it is in Isaiah 26:17-21. And there are people who were raptured before. You know who I'm talking about right? Enoch (Genesis 5:22-24) and Elijah (2 Kings 2:1-11). Enoch lived prior to the flood and walked with God so closely that one day God just took him. Elijah was a prophet who got a super cool ride into heaven in a chariot of fire.

Satan loves to make fun of the rapture. Date setters, people who think they've figured out when the rapture is going to happen, are one of his tools. When their predictions fail, people make fun of them and the entire rapture doctrine. Over time it starts to become uncool to believe in the rapture. Satan gets a little victory because he got people to stop looking for Jesus's soon return. You see, the Bible tells us we won't know the day or hour of the rapture (Matthew 24:36). It's an imminent event. It could happen any moment. That's why Jesus told us to be watching. Satan doesn't want you to know it's imminent. He wants you to think you've got plenty of time to live however you want down here on earth. That you've got plenty of time to get right with Jesus per se.

Well, you don't! That's because we absolutely can know the season of Jesus's return. He gave us many signs to watch for including signs leading up to the Antichrist's reign and the events which take place in the tribulation period. When we can see tribulation events on the horizon, we know Jesus could be here any minute! We are in the season of his return folks. There are plenty of books you can read about these signs. I'd suggest *The Book Of Signs* by Dr. David Jeremiah or *Discerners* by Terry James and other Bible prophecy experts.[2] If you'd rather watch a short video, then check out an interview that Nathan Jones, from the *Christ in Prophecy* TV show, recently did with Jan Markell regarding the top 10 prophetic signs from 2020 (https://youtu.be/IxPqYuxjmqQ).[3]

Do you know why Satan doesn't want you looking for Jesus's return at the rapture? It's because there's a special afterlife reward promised to everyone who is paying attention and looking forward to it. The apostle Paul reveals what it is.

> I have fought the good fight. I have finished the course. I have kept the faith. From now on, the crown of righteousness is stored up for me, which the Lord, the righteous judge, will give to me on that day; and not to me only, but also to all those who have loved his appearing. (2 Timothy 4:7-8)

That's right. It's a crown! The "crown of righteousness." Satan wants to steal it from you. If Satan can't prevent you from putting your faith in Jesus, then he tries to steal any treasure or rewards you might earn in heaven so that you'll feel ashamed when you get there.

This isn't a crown that people will get at Jesus's second coming. He won't be handing out crowns then. This Scripture depicts an event in the present heaven that happens right after the rapture. Jesus is about to open the scroll that starts the judgments of the tribulation period.

> They sang a new song, saying, "You are worthy to take the book and to open its seals, for you were killed, and bought us for God with your blood out of every tribe, language, people, and nation, and made us kings and priests to our God; and we will reign on the earth." (Revelation 5:9-10)

Jesus is the one who was killed and bought believers, his church, with his blood. Jesus made the believers he purchased "kings" who will "reign on the earth." Crowns are reserved for the church, people who've put their faith in Jesus since his resurrection and before his second coming. It's the church that's going to be ruling with Jesus in the millennial period. We discussed some of the other crowns mentioned in the Bible back in Chapter 7. I know this may seem a bit daunting. Perhaps you don't think you could handle ruling anything. I take comfort in knowing that Jesus will ensure we are well prepared to serve him in whatever capacity he asks us. Don't let Satan assault your afterlife by convincing you that you aren't able or aren't worthy. You can do all things through Christ (Philippians 4:13).

Crowns and rulership aren't the only rewards Jesus will be giving out. There's also treasure. Now, we're not told what this treasure is, but we can take an educated guess. Jesus told us to store our treasure in heaven instead of on earth (Matthew 6:19-21). That's because the thief, Satan, is after it. What do you consider treasure on earth? Possessions like jewelry, clothes, property. How about relationships? We consider those treasure too, don't we? We're going to be getting treasure in heaven based on what we've done here on earth (1 Corinthians 3:12-15, 2 Corinthians 5:10). You see, even though we're saved through faith, we're all expected to demonstrate our faith. This assessment of our works is called the judgment seat of Christ (Romans 14:10).

Another special reward that Satan wants to keep you from is the "wedding of the Lamb." Jesus is the "Lamb." That's right, if you've put your faith in Jesus, he considers you his bride (2 Corinthians 11:2). This wedding happens after the rapture, during the tribulation period, and before Jesus's second coming.

> "Let's rejoice and be exceedingly glad, and let's give the glory to him. For the wedding of the Lamb has come, and his wife has made herself ready." It was given to her that she would array herself in bright, pure, fine linen: for the fine linen is the righteous acts of the saints. (Revelation 19:7-8)

Have you ever been to a fancy wedding? It will pale in comparison to what Jesus has planned for his believers. We're going to get to show off our brand-new bodies, beautiful attire, and crowns to all of our family and friends who get raptured with us, who have gone before us and are already there, and all sorts of new friends that we'll meet who lived throughout the ages, including holy angels. I can see why Satan wants to keep us from this. He knows it's going to be epic!

Perhaps you hadn't given much thought to the rapture prior to reading this chapter. Maybe you figured it wasn't worth learning about or watching for because you really don't want to know if Jesus could return today. You're happy with your life on earth and you have a lot of apprehension about the afterlife anyway. You figure it doesn't matter if you're watching for him, that he'll come when he comes. You'd rather see Jesus when you're old and gray and lived a full life here. Or you want your kids to grow up and experience life first. All of those attitudes are exactly what Satan desires for you. You're letting him steal your hope and your faith in God's promises. If Satan can get you apathetic about Jesus's return to get us and all the wonderful things we just discussed, then what else has he convinced you of?

Shortly after the epic wedding, all of the people and holy angels in heaven return to earth with Jesus (Revelation 19). Jesus returns in awesome glory. There will be signs that are absolutely terrifying to people alive on earth. In the second Scripture below, Jesus is the "Son of Man."

> When the Lord Jesus is revealed from heaven with his mighty angels in flaming fire, punishing those who don't know God. (2 Thessalonians 1:7-8)

> "There will be signs in the sun, moon, and stars; and on the earth anxiety of nations, in perplexity for the roaring of the sea and the waves; men fainting for fear and for expectation of the things which are coming on the world, for the powers of the heavens will be shaken. Then they will see the Son of Man coming in a cloud with power and great glory. But when these

things begin to happen, look up and lift up your heads, because your redemption is near." (Luke 21:25-28)

Can you imagine seeing every holy angel along with all the believers? There will be millions. That's what Satan is going to see! And that's a big reason why Satan assaults the rapture, your afterlife. He doesn't want to see you in all of that glory!

Don't give him the satisfaction of keeping you from being included in the rapture, or from wearing the crown of righteousness when you return and see his demise! Instead, "look up and lift up your heads" because the King is coming!

CHAPTER 20 - ALL WILL SEE

One of the primary ways that Satan assaults the afterlife is by corrupting, defacing, and marring our beliefs about our bodies and what they'll be like in heaven. It's because we are made in the image of God. Satan doesn't want you to know that or realize how special you are because of it. Consider this. Before God created Adam, nothing else in heaven looked like Jesus. Satan, an angel, was called beautiful. I'm sure Satan and the fallen angels even mocked how different Jesus was. How plain he was compared to them and Satan. I wonder what the holy angels thought of Jesus. Did they think he was odd or just special and unique? Well, then God created Adam and I'm sure all of heaven gasped when they saw him! Adam looked like Jesus. You look like Jesus.

While we know exactly what we humans look like, we still want to know what Jesus looks like. God only tells us that Jesus isn't beautiful or majestic (Isaiah 53:2). God knew that if he gave us a complete portrait of Jesus that we'd just create an idol of him and then worship that. Or we'd try with all of our might to make ourselves look like Jesus instead of being the unique individuals he created us to be. He's keeping us from committing all sorts of sins by keeping Jesus's face hidden from us.

But one day we're all going to see his face.

> Behold, he is coming with the clouds, and every eye will see him. (Revelation 1:7)

But it's not really Jesus's face that we all desire to see. It's his glory! Moses, who talked with God for 40 years, asked God to show him his glory. But God told him that no one could see his face and live. Moses was only given a glimpse of Jesus's glory from behind (Exodus 33:18-23). It's because we're told that God lives in inapproachable light (1 Timothy 6:16). Since Moses longed to see God's glory, I think it's why he got to witness Jesus's transfiguration (Luke 9:28-31). We're all going to have a moment that's even better than the one Moses got. We're going to see Jesus in all his glory!

> I saw, in the right hand of him who sat on the throne, a book written inside and outside, sealed shut with seven seals. I saw a mighty angel proclaiming

with a loud voice, "Who is worthy to open the book, and to break its seals?" No one in heaven above, or on the earth, or under the earth, was able to open the book or to look in it. ... One of the elders said to me, "Don't weep. Behold, the Lion who is of the tribe of Judah, the Root of David, has overcome: he who opens the book and its seven seals." I saw in the middle of the throne and of the four living creatures, and in the middle of the elders, a Lamb standing, as though it had been slain, having seven horns and seven eyes, which are the seven Spirits of God, sent out into all the earth. Then he came, and he took it out of the right hand of him who sat on the throne. Now when he had taken the book... They sang a new song, saying, "You are worthy to take the book and to open its seals, for you were killed, and bought us for God with your blood out of every tribe, language, people, and nation, and made us kings and priests to our God; and we will reign on the earth." I looked, and I heard something like a voice of many angels around the throne, the living creatures, and the elders. The number of them was ten thousands of ten thousands, and thousands of thousands, saying with a loud voice, "Worthy is the Lamb who has been killed to receive the power, wealth, wisdom, strength, honor, glory, and blessing!" I heard every created thing which is in heaven, on the earth, under the earth, on the sea, and everything in them, saying, "To him who sits on the throne and to the Lamb be the blessing, the honor, the glory, and the dominion, forever and ever! Amen!" (Revelation 5:1-3, 5-13)

This event takes place in heaven right after the rapture. As a believer, you're going to be there witnessing this in your new forever body! God the father is the one "who sat on the throne." The "Lamb" is Jesus. This is when God gives Jesus the title deed per se to his entire kingdom. There is no more room in heaven for Satan because Jesus takes over! Notice how many people celebrate this glorious event. "Every created thing." You know, we're going to be in heaven witnessing this, but I wonder how this is going to manifest on earth and in the present hell. I mean it says everything worships Jesus. Do you think God will cause unbelievers who are left behind, or those who are already dead in the present hell, or even the fallen angels and demons to spontaneously shout out in praise? And what about the animals and birds and such? Is God going to open their mouth like he did for Balaam's donkey (Numbers 22:28)? It's a curious mystery indeed!

What isn't a mystery is what Jesus looks like in all of his glory.

> And among the lamp stands was one like a son of man, clothed with a robe reaching down to his feet, and with a golden sash around his chest. His head and his hair were white as white wool, like snow. His eyes were like a flame of fire. His feet were like burnished brass, as if it had been refined in a furnace. His voice was like the voice of many waters. He had seven stars in his right hand. Out of his mouth proceeded a sharp two-edged sword. His face was like the sun shining at its brightest. When I saw him, I fell at his feet like a dead man. He laid his right hand on me, saying, "Don't be afraid. I am the first and the last, and the Living one. I was dead, and behold, I am alive forever and ever. Amen. I have the keys of Death and of Hades." (Revelation 1:13-18)

We've never seen anything like him before, have we? Eyes like a flame and a face that shines like the sun. It's hard to fathom. When we see Jesus face-to-face, like his disciple John did here, we're also going to fall on our face as though dead. We won't be able to help it! We'll be awestruck. But you know what? You're not going to be on the ground for long because Jesus wants you to sit with him, on his very throne. Jesus is "I" in this Scripture.

> "He who overcomes, I will give to him to sit down with me on my throne, as I also overcame and sat down with my Father on his throne." (Revelation 3:21)

Pretty incredible, right! I find it all so overwhelming to think about. It's the ultimate rags to riches story. God loves you so much that he came to earth and died for you so that you can be with him. So that you can sit with him in heaven. Because he wants to shower you with all of his blessings for all of eternity.

Don't you see? Victory in Satan's assault against your afterlife is already yours! To God, all of these events have already happened. He knows the end from the beginning. He reveals it to us so that we can be confident in this war against our afterlife. God already won! We just have to believe him.

In the days ahead, you need to remain strong in your faith and keep your armor of God securely fastened around you (Ephesians 6:10-18). Demonstrate your faith in both your words and in your actions to keep yourself strong and equipped. While you wait for Jesus to return and reveal his glory, resist Satan and his assaults against the afterlife, and he'll go away (James 4:7). Above all, know that nothing in all of creation, not even Satan himself, can steal you, as a believer, away from God's love (Romans 8:35-39). He's holding you, and he won't let go!

Tell the people you love about God's victory, about the heavenly afterlife that's awaiting us.

> "Things which an eye didn't see, and an ear didn't hear, which didn't enter into the heart of man, these God has prepared for those who love him." (1 Corinthians 2:9)

> Now to Him who is able to [carry out His purpose and] do superabundantly more than all that we dare ask or think [infinitely beyond our greatest prayers, hopes, or dreams], according to His power that is at work within us, to Him be the glory in the church and in Christ Jesus throughout all generations forever and ever. Amen. (Ephesians 3:20-21 AMP)

What lies ahead is all so wonderful that we can't even imagine it in our hearts. It's "superabundantly more" and "infinitely beyond our greatest" thoughts.

I hope you enjoyed this journey through heaven. If you'd like to show your support for my work, please leave a review wherever you purchased this book. It's free to do, and it'll only take you a minute to write a quick sentence expressing your thoughts about the book. Your review is very important to independent, self-published authors like me. Internet and online bookstore algorithms favor books with reviews. They display in search results and at the top of search results more often than books without reviews. I even need a minimum number of reviews before I can purchase certain advertising. So, your review will help more people find this book so that they can learn all about what awaits them in heaven too. Go to rapture911.com/reviews if you need a link to where you can leave a review.

Thanks for your support!

Marsha

GET FREE BOOKS
rapture911.com/free

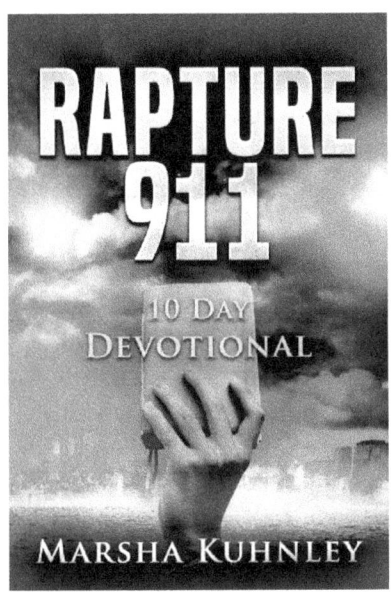

BOOKS BY MARSHA KUHNLEY

Rapture 911 Series
*Rapture 911: What To Do If You're Left Behind
Rapture 911: What To Do If You're Left Behind (Pocket Edition)
Rapture 911: 10 Day Devotional
Rapture 911: Prophecy Reference Bible

End Times Armor Series
Assault On The Afterlife: Satan's War Against Heaven
*The Election Omen: Your Vote Matters
The Election Omen: 10 Day Devotional

Other Works
Seeing The Light In Dark Times: 10 Day Devotional

Christian Sci-Fi/Fantasy
Kiara Kole And The Key Of Truth

Visit Marsha's website to find these books
rapture911.com

* - Also available as an audiobook

ABOUT THE AUTHOR

Marsha Kuhnley is an American author of Christian non-fiction books. She has a passion for Bible prophecy, finance, and economics. You may have seen Marsha as a guest on the popular *Christ In Prophecy* TV program where she discusses her books, the Rapture, and End Times topics. She received her MBA in Finance and BA in Economics from the University of New Mexico. Prior to becoming an author, she enjoyed a career at Intel Corporation. She uses her education and career experience to take complex biblical information and present it in easily understandable concepts. You'll benefit from over a decade of her research and study of the Bible, Bible prophecy, and Rapture theology. She lives in Albuquerque, NM with her husband where they attend Calvary Church.

CONNECT WITH MARSHA

rapture911.com/connect

ENDNOTES

Chapter 1
[1] J. Barton Payne, *Encyclopedia Of Biblical Prophecy*, (Grand Rapids, MI: Baker Book House, 1973), 681.
[2] Marsha Kuhnley, *Rapture 911: What To Do If You're Left Behind*, (Albuquerque, NM: Drezhn Publishing LLC, 2019), Part 6.
[3] Jack Langford, "Lucifer: Son Of The Dawn-Part 1," *The Prophecy Watcher*, 01.2021, 22.
Jack Langford, "Creation Of Lucifer-Part 2," *The Prophecy Watcher*, 02.2021, 22.
Jack Langford, "Lucifer's Position-Part 3," *The Prophecy Watcher*, 03.2021, 22.
Jack Langford, "Lucifer's Judgment-Part 4," *The Prophecy Watcher*, 04.2021, 22.

Chapter 2
[1] "The Wizard of Oz (1939 film)," Wikipedia.org, https://en.wikipedia.org/wiki/The_Wizard_of_Oz_(1939_film), accessed October 9, 2021.

Chapter 4
[1] "Propaganda," Britannica.com, https://www.britannica.com/topic/propaganda, accessed September 8, 2021.
[2] Erin Perri, "Matthew McConaughey Dishes Dirt On Hollywood's Christian Bigotry," *TheMix.net*, October 26, 2020, https://www.themix.net/2020/10/matthew-mcconaughey-dishes-dirt-on-hollywoods-christian-bigotry/, accessed September 8, 2021.
[3] Eric Bailey, "Why Is There So Much Hell In Video Games And So Little Heaven?," *Love Thy Nerd*, October 4, 2018, https://lovethynerd.com/why-is-there-so-much-hell-in-video-games-and-so-little-heaven/, accessed September 8, 2021.
[4] Lucas Hill-Paul, "Lucifer Smashes Netflix Ratings As Tom Ellis Series Gains Over 1 Billion Views," *Express*, June 28, 2021, https://www.express.co.uk/showbiz/tv-radio/1455777/Lucifer-season-5-part-2-viewers-1-billion-minutes-watched-Tom-Ellis-Netflix-video-ont, accessed September 8, 2021.
[5] Laura Turner, " 'The Good Place' Has Created A Heaven And Hell Perfect For Our Time," *The Washington Post*, January 24, 2019, https://www.washingtonpost.com/religion/2019/01/24/good-place-has-created-heaven-hell-perfect-our-time/, accessed September 8, 2021.
[6] Felix Richter, "The Generation Gap In TV Consumption," *Statista*, November 20, 2020, https://www.statista.com/chart/15224/daily-tv-consumption-by-us-adults/, accessed September 8, 2021.
[7] "The Good Place," Wikipedia.org, https://en.wikipedia.org/wiki/The_Good_Place, accessed September 8, 2021.
[8] "Lucifer (TV series)," Wikipedia.org, https://en.wikipedia.org/wiki/Lucifer_(TV_series), accessed September 8, 2021.
[9] "Upload (TV series)," Wikipedia.org, https://en.wikipedia.org/wiki/Upload_(TV_series), accessed September 8, 2021.
[10] "Self/less," Wikipedia.org, https://en.wikipedia.org/wiki/Self/less, accessed September 8, 2021.
[11] "Star Wars," Wikipedia.org, https://en.wikipedia.org/wiki/Star_Wars, accessed October 4, 2021.
[12] "Death," Starwars.fandom.com, https://starwars.fandom.com/wiki/Death,

accessed September 8, 2021.
[13] "The Sixth Sense," Wikipedia.org, https://en.wikipedia.org/wiki/The_Sixth_Sense, accessed September 8, 2021.
[14] Alex Zhavoronkov, PhD, "Elon Musk's Big Neuralink Paper: Should We Prepare For The Digital Afterlife?," *Forbes*, June 17, 2021, https://www.forbes.com/sites/alexzhavoronkov/2021/06/17/elon-musks-big-neuralink-paper-should-we-prepare-for-the-digital-afterlife/?sh=7cb969cd554d, accessed September 8, 2021.
[15] Martine Paris, "Deepak Chopra And Richard Branson To Live On Forever Through AI, Here's How," *Forbes*, June 4, 2021, https://www.forbes.com/sites/martineparis/2021/06/04/deepak-chopra-plans-to-live-forever-through-ai-heres-how/?sh=782492f04871, accessed August 28, 2021.
[16] Arjun Kharpal, "Elon Musk: Humans Must Merge With Machines Or Become Irrelevant In AI Age," *CNBC*, February 13, 2017, https://www.cnbc.com/2017/02/13/elon-musk-humans-merge-machines-cyborg-artificial-intelligence-robots.html, accessed September 8, 2021.
[17] Adam Eliyahu Berkowitz, "Scientists Propose Surrounding The Sun With Supercomputer To Resurrect The Dead," *Israel 365 News*, March 21, 2021, https://www.israel365news.com/188609/scientists-propose-surrounding-the-sun-with-supercomputer-to-resurrect-the-dead/, accessed September 8, 2021.

Chapter 5

[1] Randy Alcorn, *Heaven*, (Carol Stream, IL: Tyndale House Publishers, Inc., 2004).
[2] "Is The Bible Trustworthy As A Historical Document?," CARM.org, https://carm.org/is-the-bible-trustworthy-as-a-historical-document, accessed October 1, 2021.
[3] Marsha Kuhnley, *Rapture 911: What To Do If You're Left Behind*, (Albuquerque, NM: Drezhn Publishing LLC, 2019), Part 5 and Part 6.
[4] "Imagine Lyrics," AZlyrics.com, https://www.azlyrics.com/lyrics/johnlennon/imagine.html, accessed September 2, 2021.
[5] Ian Sample, "Stephen Hawking: 'There Is No Heaven; It's A Fairy Story'," *The Guardian*, May 15, 2011, https://www.theguardian.com/science/2011/may/15/stephen-hawking-interview-there-is-no-heaven, accessed September 2, 2021.
[6] Dave Courvoisier, "Is There Life After Death? Las Vegas Businessman Offering Nearly $1M For Evidence," *KTNV Las Vegas*, February 15, 2021, https://www.ktnv.com/news/is-there-life-after-death-las-vegas-businessman-offering-nearly-1m-to-anyone-with-evidence, accessed September 2, 2021.
"BICS Contest," BigelowInstitute.org, https://www.bigelowinstitute.org/contest.php, accessed September 2, 2021.
[7] "What Happens After We Die?," *Today*, October 6, 2006, https://www.today.com/popculture/what-happens-after-we-die-wbna15291472, accessed September 2, 2021.
[8] "Defending Your Life," Wikipedia.org, https://en.wikipedia.org/wiki/Defending_Your_Life, accessed October 4, 2021.
[9] "Good Omens (TV series)," Wikipedia.org, https://en.wikipedia.org/wiki/Good_Omens_(TV_series), accessed October 4, 2021.
"The Good Place," Wikipedia.org, https://en.wikipedia.org/wiki/The_Good_Place, accessed September 8, 2021.
"Soul (2020 film)," Wikipedia.org,

https://en.wikipedia.org/wiki/Soul_(2020_film), accessed October 4, 2021.
10 "Lucifer (TV series)," Wikipedia.org, https://en.wikipedia.org/wiki/Lucifer_(TV_series), accessed September 8, 2021.

Chapter 6
1 Burning Man Project, https://burningman.org/, accessed September 4, 2021.
2 "What Is Midburn?," Midburn.org, https://en.midburn.org/whats-midburn, accessed September 4, 2021.
3 "All About Zozobra," BurnZozobra.com, https://burnzozobra.com/about/, accessed September 4, 2021.
4 "Timeline," Burningman.org, https://burningman.org/timeline/, accessed September 4, 2021.
5 "What Is The Temple?," TempleGuardians.com, https://templeguardians.burningman.org/about-the-temples/, accessed September 4, 2021.
6 Carl Teichrib, *Game of Gods: The Temple of Man in the Age of Re-Enchantment*, Kindle Edition, (Whitemud House Publishing, 2018), Chapter 14, Endnote 1714.
7 Ken Johnson, Th.D., *Ancient Book of Jubilees*, Kindle Edition, (USA: Biblefacts Ministries, 2013), Chapter 10:21.
8 "List Of Tallest Buildings," Wikipedia.org, https://en.wikipedia.org/wiki/List_of_tallest_buildings, accessed September 4, 2021.
9 Ken Johnson, Th.D., *Ancient Book of Jasher*, Kindle Edition, (USA: Biblefacts Ministries, 2013), Chapter 9:25.

Chapter 7
1 "The Great Reset," WEForum.org, https://www.weforum.org/great-reset/, accessed September 15, 2021.
2 "Now Is The Time For A 'Great Reset'," WEForum.org, https://www.weforum.org/agenda/2020/06/now-is-the-time-for-a-great-reset/, accessed September 6, 2021.

Chapter 8
1 Ken Johnson, Th.D., *Ancient Church Fathers*, Kindle Edition, (USA: 2010), See Astral Projection, Page 146.
2 Ken Johnson, Th.D., *Ancient Book of Enoch*, Kindle Edition, (USA: 2012), Enoch Chapter 15:8, Page 29. Appendix B, Jubilees 10:1-12.

Chapter 9
1 https://en.wikipedia.org/wiki/Day_of_the_Dead "Day Of The Dead," Wikipedia.org, https://en.wikipedia.org/wiki/Day_of_the_Dead , accessed September 15, 2021.
2 "Coco (2017 film)," Wikipedia.org, https://en.wikipedia.org/wiki/Coco_(2017_film), accessed October 4, 2021.
3 "Purgatory," Catholic.com, https://www.catholic.com/encyclopedia/purgatory, accessed September 15, 2021.

Chapter 10
1 Ken Johnson, Th.D., *Ancient Paganism*, Kindle Edition, (USA: 2009), See The Coming of a New Age, The Secret, Page 140.
2 John Jalsevac, "The World's "Most Dangerous" Spiritual Guru: Oprah Begins 10-

Week Online New Age Class," *LifeSiteNews.com*, March 7, 2008, https://www.lifesitenews.com/news/the-worlds-most-dangerous-spiritual-guru-oprah-begins-10-week-online-new-ag/, accessed September 15, 2021.

3 Eckhart Tolle, "Eckhart On The Meaning Of Christmas," *Tolle Teachings* (blog), http://tolleteachings.com/eckhart-on-Christmas.html, accessed September 15, 2021.

Chapter 11

1 "The Walking Dead (TV series)," Wikipedia.org, https://en.wikipedia.org/wiki/The_Walking_Dead_(TV_series), accessed September 18, 2021.

2 "Resident Evil," Wikipedia.org, https://en.wikipedia.org/wiki/Resident_Evil, accessed September 18, 2021.

3 "Bram Stoker's Dracula (1992 film)," Wikipedia.org, https://en.wikipedia.org/wiki/Bram_Stoker%27s_Dracula_(1992_film), accessed October 4, 2021.

"The Twilight Saga (film series)," Wikipedia.org, https://en.wikipedia.org/wiki/The_Twilight_Saga_(film_series), accessed October 4, 2021.

"Supernatural (American TV series)," Wikipedia.org, https://en.wikipedia.org/wiki/Supernatural_(American_TV_series), accessed October 4, 2021.

"Buffy the Vampire Slayer," Wikipedia.org, https://en.wikipedia.org/wiki/Buffy_the_Vampire_Slayer, accessed October 4, 2021.

"Interview with the Vampire (film)," Wikipedia.org, https://en.wikipedia.org/wiki/Interview_with_the_Vampire_(film), accessed October 4, 2021.

4 Rebecca Jennings, "Ghosts, Witches, Zombies: Which Supernatural Creature Makes The Most Money At The Box Office?," *Vox*, October 21, 2018, https://www.vox.com/the-goods/2018/10/29/18018906/ghost-witch-zombie-movie-box-office, accessed September 18, 2021.

5 Matthew Shaer, "Scientists Are Giving Dead Brains New Life. What Could Go Wrong?," *The New York Times Magazine*, July 2, 2019, https://www.nytimes.com/2019/07/02/magazine/dead-pig-brains-reanimation.html, accessed September 18, 2021.

6 Kate Sheridan, "Resurrected: A Controversial Trial To Bring The Dead Back To Life," *Scientific American*, June 1, 2017, https://www.scientificamerican.com/article/resurrected-a-controversial-trial-to-bring-the-dead-back-to-life/, accessed September 18, 2021.

7 Michael Greshko, "Pig Brains Partially Revived Hours After Death - What It Means For People," *National Geographic*, April 17, 2019, https://www.nationalgeographic.com/science/article/pig-brains-partially-revived-what-it-means-for-medicine-death-ethics, accessed September 18, 2021.

8 Adam Piore, "Can Blood From Young People Slow Aging? Silicon Valley Has Bet Billions It Will," *Newsweek*, April 7, 2021, https://www.newsweek.com/2021/04/16/can-blood-young-people-slow-aging-silicon-valley-has-bet-billions-it-will-1581447.html, accessed September 18, 2021.

Chapter 12

1 "The Matrix," Wikipedia.org, https://en.wikipedia.org/wiki/The_Matrix, accessed October 4, 2021.

2. "Free Guy," Wikipedia.org, https://en.wikipedia.org/wiki/Free_Guy, accessed October 4, 2021.
3. Corey S. Powell, "Elon Musk Says We May Live In A Simulation. Here's How We Might Tell If He's Right," *NBC News*, October 2, 2018, https://www.nbcnews.com/mach/science/what-simulation-hypothesis-why-some-think-life-simulated-reality-ncna913926, accessed September 23, 2021.
4. Corey S. Powell, "Elon Musk Says We May Live In A Simulation. Here's How We Might Tell If He's Right," *NBC News*, October 2, 2018, https://www.nbcnews.com/mach/science/what-simulation-hypothesis-why-some-think-life-simulated-reality-ncna913926, accessed September 23, 2021.
5. Rizwan Virk, "Religion And The Simulation Hypothesis: Is God An AI (Part I)?," *Hackernoon*, March 31, 2019, https://hackernoon.com/religion-and-the-simulation-hypothesis-is-god-an-ai-part-i-e2ac0016ca1e, accessed September 23, 2021.
6. Sean Illing, "Are We Living In A Computer Simulation? I Don't Know. Probably.," *Vox*, October 24, 2020, https://www.vox.com/future-perfect/2019/4/10/18275618/simulation-hypothesis-matrix-rizwan-virk, accessed September 23, 2021.
7. Anil Ananthaswamy, "Do We Live In A Simulation? Chances Are About 50-50," *Scientific American*, October 13, 2020, https://www.scientificamerican.com/article/do-we-live-in-a-simulation-chances-are-about-50-50/, accessed September 23, 2021.
8. Matt Strieb, "15 Irrefutable Reasons Why We Might Be Living In A Simulation," *Vulture*, February 2, 2019, https://www.vulture.com/2019/02/15-irrefutable-reasons-we-might-be-living-in-a-simulation.html, accessed September 23, 2021.
9. Brian Feldman, "Philosopher Nick Bostrom On Whether We Live In A Simulation," *Vulture*, February 6, 2019, https://www.vulture.com/2019/02/nick-bostrom-on-whether-we-live-in-a-matrix-simulation.html, accessed September 22, 2021.
10. https://fossbytes.com/most-realistic-games/ Akshay Bhardwaj, "7 Most Realistic Games With Outstanding Graphics & Gameplay In 2021," *Fossbytes*, April 8, 2021, https://fossbytes.com/most-realistic-games/ , accessed September 23, 2021.
11. "Berenstain Bears," Wikipedia.org, https://en.wikipedia.org/wiki/Berenstain_Bears, accessed October 4, 2021.
12. Latchesar Ionkov, Bradley Settlemyer, "DNA: The Ultimate Data-Storage Solution," *Scientific American*, May 28, 2021, https://www.scientificamerican.com/article/dna-the-ultimate-data-storage-solution/, accessed September 22, 2021.
13. "Gifts Of State," Archives.gov, https://www.archives.gov/exhibits/tokens_and_treasures/gifts_of_state.html, accessed September 23, 2021.

Chapter 13
1. "Back to the Future," Wikipedia.org, https://en.wikipedia.org/wiki/Back_to_the_Future, accessed October 4, 2021.
2. Matthew S. Schwartz, "Paradox-Free Time Travel Is Theoretically Possible, Researchers Say," *NPR*, September 27, 2020, https://www.npr.org/2020/09/27/917556254/paradox-free-time-travel-is-theoretically-possible-researchers-say, accessed September 23, 2021.
3. Susie Neilson, "Time Travel Is Theoretically Possible, New Calculations Show. But That Doesn't Mean You Could Change The Past.," *Business Insider*, September 30, 2020, https://www.businessinsider.com/time-travel-possible-changing-past-isnt-physics-says-2020-9, accessed September 23, 2021.

4 "We Can Build A Real Time Machine'," *BBC*, July 11, 2018, https://www.bbc.com/news/science-environment-44771942, accessed September 23, 2021.
5 Cathal O'Connell, "Time Travel: Five Ways That We Could Do It," *Cosmos Magazine*, August 3, 2021, https://cosmosmagazine.com/science/physics/five-ways-to-travel-through-time/, accessed September 23, 2021.
6 George F.R. Ellis, "Why The Multiverse May Be The Most Dangerous Idea In Physics," *Scientific American*, August 2014, https://www.scientificamerican.com/article/why-the-multiverse-may-be-the-most-dangerous-idea-in-physics/, accessed September 23, 2021.
7 Ethan Siegel, "This Is Why The Multiverse Must Exist," *Forbes*, March 15, 2019, https://www.forbes.com/sites/startswithabang/2019/03/15/this-is-why-the-multiverse-must-exist/?sh=5fff50826d08, accessed September 23, 2021.
8 Clara Moskowitz, "5 Reasons We May Live In A Multiverse," *Space.com*, December 7, 2012, https://www.space.com/18811-multiple-universes-5-theories.html, accessed September 23, 2021.
9 Eugene Lim, "The Theory Of Parallel Universes Is Not Just Maths - It Is Science That Can Be Tested," *Phys.org*, September 3, 2015, https://phys.org/news/2015-09-theory-parallel-universes-maths-science.html, accessed September 23, 2021.
10 "Spider-Man: Into the Spider-Verse," Wikipedia.org, https://en.wikipedia.org/wiki/Spider-Man:_Into_the_Spider-Verse, accessed October 4, 2021.
11 Eugene Lim, "The Theory Of Parallel Universes Is Not Just Maths - It Is Science That Can Be Tested," *Phys.org*, September 3, 2015, https://phys.org/news/2015-09-theory-parallel-universes-maths-science.html, accessed September 23, 2021.
Clara Moskowitz, "5 Reasons We May Live In A Multiverse," *Space.com*, December 7, 2012, https://www.space.com/18811-multiple-universes-5-theories.html, accessed September 23, 2021.
Vicky Stein, "Do Parallel Universes Exist? We Might Live In A Multiverse.," *Space.com*, June 8, 2021, https://www.space.com/32728-parallel-universes.html, accessed September 23, 2021.
Ethan Siegel, "This Is Why The Multiverse Must Exist," *Forbes*, March 15, 2019, https://www.forbes.com/sites/startswithabang/2019/03/15/this-is-why-the-multiverse-must-exist/?sh=5fff50826d08, accessed September 23, 2021.

Chapter 14
1 "The Transhumanist Manifesto," HumanityPlus.org, https://humanityplus.org/transhumanism/transhumanist-manifesto/, accessed September 25, 2021.
2 Neuralink, https://neuralink.com/, accessed September 25, 2021.
3 Cryonics Institute, https://www.cryonics.org/, accessed September 25, 2021.
4 "Inspector Gadget," Wikipedia.org, https://en.wikipedia.org/wiki/Inspector_Gadget, accessed October 10, 2021.
5 Arjun Kharpal, "Elon Musk: Humans Must Merge With Machines Or Become Irrelevant In AI Age," *CNBC*, February 13, 2017, https://www.cnbc.com/2017/02/13/elon-musk-humans-merge-machines-cyborg-artificial-intelligence-robots.html, accessed September 25, 2021.
6 Nirmal Narayanan, "Human Immortality: Will Harvard's Genetic Reset Trials Help Us Live Forever?," *International Business Times*, June 9, 2021, https://www.ibtimes.co.in/human-immortality-will-harvards-genetic-reset-trials-help-us-live-forever-837331, accessed September 25, 2021.
7 Michael Moran, "New Blood, Computer Brains And Frozen Heads: How

Billionaires 'Will Live Forever'," *Daily Star*, September 19, 2020, https://www.dailystar.co.uk/news/weird-news/new-blood-computer-brains-frozen-22695138, accessed September 25, 2021.

[8] Anna Savva, "Peter The Human Cyborg's Mind-Blowing Journey To 'Cheat Death' As Part Man, Part Machine," *Daily Star*, August 26, 2020, https://www.dailystar.co.uk/news/latest-news/scientist-embarks-mind-blowing-journey-22584258, accessed September 25, 2021.

[9] Tyler Durden, "Transhumanism: The New Religion Of The Coming Technocracy," *ZeroHedge*, June 23, 2020, https://www.zerohedge.com/technology/transhumanism-new-religion-coming-technocracy, accessed September 25, 2021.

[10] Victor Tangermann, "Elon Musk Mocks Jeff Bezos' Attempt To Develop Immortality Tech," *Futurism*, September 7, 2021, https://futurism.com/elon-musk-mocks-jeff-bezos-immortality-tech, accessed September 25, 2021.

[11] "The Philosophy of Transhumanism," HumanityPlus.org, https://humanityplus.org/transhumanism/philosophy-of-transhumanism/, accessed September 25, 2021.

[12] Ken Johnson, Th.D., *Ancient Book of Jasher*, Kindle Edition, (USA: Biblefacts Ministries, 2013), Chapter 6:14-23.

[13] "The Philosophy Of Transhumanism," HumanityPlus.org, https://humanityplus.org/transhumanism/philosophy-of-transhumanism/, accessed September 25, 2021.

Chapter 15

[1] "Ready Player One (film)," Wikipedia.org, https://en.wikipedia.org/wiki/Ready_Player_One_(film), accessed September 25, 2021.

[2] Casey Newton, "Mark In The Metaverse," *The Verge*, July 22, 2021, https://www.theverge.com/22588022/mark-zuckerberg-facebook-ceo-metaverse-interview, accessed September 25, 2021.

[3] Mitchell Clark, "NFTs, Explained," *The Verge*, August 18, 2021, https://www.theverge.com/22310188/nft-explainer-what-is-blockchain-crypto-art-faq, accessed September 25, 2021.

[4] "The Philosophy Of Transhumanism," HumanityPlus.org, https://humanityplus.org/transhumanism/philosophy-of-transhumanism/, accessed September 25, 2021.

[5] "Upload (TV series)," Wikipedia.org, https://en.wikipedia.org/wiki/Upload_(TV_series), accessed September 8, 2021.

[6] Alex Zhavoronkov, PhD, "Elon Musk's Big Neuralink Paper: Should We Prepare For The Digital Afterlife?," *Forbes*, June 17, 2021, https://www.forbes.com/sites/alexzhavoronkov/2021/06/17/elon-musks-big-neuralink-paper-should-we-prepare-for-the-digital-afterlife/?sh=7cb969cd554d, accessed August 28, 2021.

[7] Sebastian Kettley, "Life After death: Physicist Michio Kaku Says Digital Immortaility Is 'Within Reach'," *Express*, March 23, 2021, https://www.express.co.uk/news/science/1386273/life-after-death-michio-kaku-digital-immortality-afterlife-evg, accessed September 27, 2021.

[8] Martine Paris, "Deepak Chopra And Richard Branson To Live On Forever Through AI, Here's How," *Forbes*, June 4, 2021, https://www.forbes.com/sites/martineparis/2021/06/04/deepak-chopra-plans-to-live-forever-through-ai-heres-how/?sh=782492f04871, accessed September 27, 2021.

9 Asa Fitch, "Could AI Keep People 'Alive' After Death?," *The Wall Street Journal*, July 3, 2021, https://www.wsj.com/articles/could-ai-keep-people-alive-after-death-11625317200, accessed August 28, 2021.
10 Dan Robitzski, "The Digital Afterlife Is Open For Business. But It Needs Rules.," *Futurism*, April 18, 2018, https://futurism.com/companies-digital-afterlife-ethical-guidelines, accessed August 28, 2021.
11 "J.A.R.V.I.S.," Wikipedia.org, https://en.wikipedia.org/wiki/J.A.R.V.I.S., accessed October 4, 2021.

Chapter 16

1 Ryan Pitterson, *Judgment Of The Nephilim*, Kindle Edition, (New York, NY: Days Of Noe Publishing, 2017).
2 "CRISPR/Cas9," Crisprtx.com, http://www.crisprtx.com/gene-editing/crispr-cas9, accessed September 21, 2021.
3 Ashley Sadler, "US Senate Passes Bill To Give Billions Of Dollars In Funding For Human-Animal Hybrid Experiments," *LifeSiteNews.com*, June 14, 2021, https://www.lifesitenews.com/news/us-senate-passes-bill-to-give-billions-of-dollars-in-funding-for-human-animal-hybrid-experiments/, accessed September 21, 2021.
4 Nathaniel Scharping, "Why Scientists Have Been Creating Chimeras In The Lab For Decades," *Discover Magazine*, May 19, 2021, https://www.discovermagazine.com/health/why-scientists-have-been-creating-chimeras-in-the-lab-for-decades, accessed September 21, 2021.
5 Maija Palmer, Tim Smith, "Startups Are Helping Armies Create Legions Of Super-Soldiers," *Sifted*, August 5, 2021, https://sifted.eu/articles/startups-super-soldiers/, accessed September 21, 2021.
6 Adam Eliyahu Berkowitz, "Researchers Inject Human DNA Into Monkeys, Recreating Pre-Flood Sin Of The 'Nephilim'," *Israel 365 News*, November 30, 2020, https://www.israel365news.com/161463/researchers-inject-human-dna-into-monkeys-recreating-pre-flood-sin-of-the-nephilim/, accessed September 21, 2021.
7 David Cyranoski, "Japan Approves First Human-Animal Embryo Experiments," *Nature*, July 26, 2019, https://www.nature.com/articles/d41586-019-02275-3, accessed September 21, 2021.
8 Peter Dockrill, "Scientists Successfully Made Sheep-Human Hybrids In 2018," *Science Alert*, January 1, 2019, https://www.sciencealert.com/scientists-successfully-made-sheep-human-hybrids-in-2018, accessed September 21, 2021.
9 Maayan Jaffe-Hoffman, "Israeli Doctors Develop 'Pig-Human' Hybrid Organ For Transplant," *The Jerusalem Post*, April 7, 2021, https://www.jpost.com/health-science/israeli-doctors-develop-pig-human-hybrid-organ-for-transplant-672861, accessed September 21, 2021.
10 "Sweet Tooth (TV series)," Wikipedia.org, https://en.wikipedia.org/wiki/Sweet_Tooth_(TV_series), accessed October 4, 2021.
11 "Ancient Aliens," Wikipedia.org, https://en.wikipedia.org/wiki/Ancient_Aliens, accessed September 21, 2021.
12 "Star Wars," Wikipedia.org, https://en.wikipedia.org/wiki/Star_Wars, accessed October 4, 2021.
"Star Trek," Wikipedia.org, https://en.wikipedia.org/wiki/Star_Trek, accessed October 4, 2021.
"E.T. the Extra-Terrestrial," Wikipedia.org, https://en.wikipedia.org/wiki/E.T._the_Extra-Terrestrial, accessed October 4, 2021.

"Stargate," Wikipedia.org, https://en.wikipedia.org/wiki/Stargate, accessed October 4, 2021.

[13] Marsha Kuhnley, *Rapture 911: What To Do If You're Left Behind*, (Albuquerque, NM: Drezhn Publishing LLC, 2019), Chapter 14.

[14] Tyler Durden, "How Genetically Similar Are We To Other Life-Forms," *ZeroHedge*, September 17, 2021, https://www.zerohedge.com/medical/how-genetically-similar-are-we-other-life-forms, accessed September 21, 2021.

Chapter 17

[1] Katherine J. Wu, "This Spiky Patch Could Invisibly Record Vaccination History Under Skin," *Smithsonian Magazine*, December 18, 2019, https://www.smithsonianmag.com/innovation/spiky-patch-could-invisibly-record-vaccination-history-under-skin-180973809/, accessed September 21, 2021.

[2] Sang Yup Lee, "DNA Data Storage Is Closer Than You Think," *Scientific American*, July 1, 2019, https://www.scientificamerican.com/article/dna-data-storage-is-closer-than-you-think/, accessed September 21, 2021.

Chapter 18

[1] "Paradise Matrix," Matrix.fandom.com, https://matrix.fandom.com/wiki/Paradise_Matrix, accessed September 12, 2021.

Chapter 19

[1] Marsha Kuhnley, *Rapture 911: What To Do If You're Left Behind*, (Albuquerque, NM: Drezhn Publishing LLC, 2019).

[2] Dr. David Jeremiah, *The Book Of Signs*, Kindle Edition, (Nashville, TN: W Publishing, 2019).

Terry James, *Discerners: Analyzing Converging Prophetic Signs For The End Of Days*, Kindle Edition, (Benton, AR: RR Press, 2019).

[3] Nathan Jones and Jan Markell, "10 Top Prophetic Trends: Prophetic Perspectives 148," March 9, 2021, *Christ In Prophecy*, video, 9:19, https://youtu.be/IxPqYuxjmqQ.

www.ingramcontent.com/pod-product-compliance
Lightning Source LLC
Chambersburg PA
CBHW062142280426
43673CB00072B/118